Naz Bah Ei Bijei:
The Heart of a Warrior

By Paul Kyle
Edited by Samuel F. Sandoval, Malula Sandoval & Sheryl Kyle

© Copy Right: 2019

ISBN 978-1-7338178-0-6

CONTENTS

Chapter 1: The Navajo Way 5

Chapter 2: School 17

Chapter 3: The Navajo Language was used to Defeat the Enemy 30

Chapter 4: Healing and Purpose 47

Chapter 5: Legacy 58

This book is dedicated to:

Samuel's Parents:

The late Julian Sandoval, Jr. (father)
The late Helen S. Sandoval (mother)

Malula's Parents:

The late Don Lee (father)
The late Bessie Lee (mother)

Samuel's wife, Malula M. Sandoval

Samuel and Malula's godchild, Kenneth Don Lee (nephew to Malula)

Preface

The vision for *The Heart of a Warrior*, the story of Samuel F. Sandoval, began at dinner on Veterans Day, 2011, in Overland Park, Kansas. Samuel had just finished speaking at several events at Johnson County Community College as a part of the college's Veteran's Week events, which I had helped to organize. A local restaurant owner asked Samuel and his wife, Malula, plus my family and I to join them for dinner. As the owner of the restaurant and Sam were engaged in a lengthy conversation, Malula, who is known by the Code Talkers in their area as their archivist, began to share how she was concerned about the preservation of her vast assortment of documents, films, videos and other items pertaining to the history of the Code Talkers. As the conversation progressed, I explained that with the vast resources of the college, maybe we could help her with this important project and, in exchange, we could have copies for our library. She said she would visit with Sam and let us know. As I thought about this idea a few days later, I became excited for this once-in-a-lifetime opportunity to broaden the scope of this relationship and to thoroughly tell Samuel's story. It did not take much to convince the president of the college, the directors of the Native American Studies program on campus, and the video production team to embark on the ambitious journey to produce a documentary about the amazing life of this man. I called Sam and Malula and asked them to consider a partnership with JCCC and, after much discussion and prayer on their part, they agreed. Many hours were spent with Samuel in our JCCC studio as he told his story in both the Navajo and

English languages. We were also able to preserve Malula's Code Talker treasures in digital form. To make the documentary, a crew traveled to Shiprock, Arizona, Farmington, New Mexico, and other places in the Four Corners region to film on location. The college is fortunate to have hours of edited and unedited videos that tell Sam and Malula's story. The documentary, *The Heart of a Warrior*, had its premiere in 2012 and was honored with a Telley Award in 2014. Following the making of the documentary, Sam requested that a book be written and he asked me to write it. The book contains stories from the documentary and from the hours and hours of conversations Sam and I have had over the years, plus a few tales from the making of the film. This book is a tribute to Samuel, his family, the Navajo Nation and the Navajo Code Talkers who faithfully served the their people and the United States in World War II.

The Heart of a Warrior

By Paul Kyle

Chapter One

'The Navajo Way'

As we approached the beach landing, the ride rocked me into a daydream-like state. Unlike my other landings at Bougainville and Guam, when the adrenaline was pumping in my bloodstream at such a fast rate that by the time I reached the beach I was exhausted, this landing felt different. This time I guess my body had caught up to the realities of war and my reaction was relatively calm and relaxed until the right time. At one point, amidst the motion of the boat, the mist and the sounds of the engine, and the salt water sloshing against the bow of the craft, I found myself closing my eyes and remembering riding my horse on the peaceful mesas of my grandmother's ranch. It was as though my body instinctively knew when I would need all my skills, knowledge and intuition to work in concert in order to stay alive and help save the lives of my fellow marines. But for now my body responded in a relaxed, restful state as my hand grasped the decorative Navajo leather pouch, the corn pollen pouch, given to me by my grandmother as I left on the bus that would take me and eight other Code Talkers to the Marine

Recruiting Depot in San Diego, California, and then on to Camp Pendleton. Suddenly the front of the boat opened up. I prepared to jump off to meet my enemy, like a mountain lion crouches down immediately before he confronts a threat to his territory. As I leaped off of the boat into the waist-deep, salty water, all of my senses were shocked into a heightened awareness and response mode. As I struggled to wade to any resemblance of safety awaiting on the beach, I had to ignore the mortar explosions and what appeared to be rain splashing up the water, but what was actually bullets hitting the water all around me. Finally after struggling through the carnage in the water, I found myself maneuvering over and around the lifeless body of one of my fellow Marines. The words of my great-grandfather came to my consciousness as though he was standing right beside me, "Do not step over dead bodies and do not touch human blood" - neither of which I could avoid because the space on the beach was too small and the devastation was too large to accommodate my childhood mentor's wise advice. I was fearful of the spiritual implication of not being able to avoid the dead and the carnage I was standing in. (Memories from Peleliu landing)

These words from his great-grandfather would not be the only words that came to Samuel F. Sandoval's mind at unusual times and under life-threatening circumstances. The fact that these and thousands of other utterances from his great-grandfather, Hostien Cly, also known as "Left Handed Man", engulfed his consciousness and subconscious mind validates the powerful influence this warrior, medicine man, and honorable Navajo had on Samuel.

Samuel, now in his nineties, recalls how his great-grandfather, who lived to be 109, was very involved in his upbringing during his early childhood. His fundamental years of development were shaped and solidified through countless hours of time spent with this influential medicine man in a nearby sweat lodge. He refers to these times as "the way of the elders." Reflecting on those cherished moments in the sweat lodge, a list of qualities imperative in a warrior resonates in his mind like a broken record. Samuel recalls his great-grandfather waking him up at four in the morning, so they could go to this personal, sacred place of worship for prayer time. His great-grandfather would say, "Don't sleep when the sun rises. If you do, poverty will take over your life. There is work to do. Let's go to the sweat lodge." He remembers getting up, wiping the sleep out of his eyes and yawning as he buttoned up his white shirt, slipped into his denim overalls and pulled on his cowboy boots. He then put on his cowboy hat, grabbed the wool blanket that had been made by one of his relatives, and followed his great-grandfather to the mysterious sweat lodge just a quarter mile from his grandmother's Hogan. His great-grandfather would remind him, "The language is sacred. Too sacred for you at this time. It might disrupt the ceremony if you say something bad, so just be quiet and listen. This way you will learn." Samuel sat quietly in his favorite place in "the traditional Navajo way," a term Samuel consistently uses when telling historical and cultural stories of his people. He sat and patiently watched his great-grandfather go through his methodical routine of preparing the sacred items and starting the small fire necessary for this time of song, prayer and storytelling. Sam's instructions were to sit quietly and to shake the gourd during the singing portions of the ceremony. On occasion, the young Samuel would fight fatigue causing his wise mentor to change his strategy by encouraging Samuel to become actively engaged in the ceremony. Samuel recalls his great-grandfather waking him when he would start to fall asleep by saying, "Wake up! Keep going, speak good words, pray good. Let your prayers be heard to the heavens…across the waters. Sing to these places. People of all walks of life are listening, that's why you speak good for them." This respected elder of the tribe needed to make sure Samuel would not forget the qualities necessary in a Navajo warrior. This "great warrior" was not the pulp-fiction or Hollywood version. The characteristics of a true Navajo warrior reach beyond the honor and bravery found when battling one's enemy. Samuel's great-grandfather did battle the U.S. Calvary (known as "blue coats" to the Navajo), which required skills in weaponry, communication, tactical strategies, reconnaissance and hand-to-hand combat – just a few of the skills needed to be a warrior. These memories his grandfather shared with him of battles with the bluecoats did, in fact, aid Samuel in his own battles with the Japanese as a fighting Marine in World War II. But Sam also learned that being a warrior was more about wisdom than brawn and strength. A warrior is more clearly defined in the context of the tribe, rather than the individual according to his great-grandfather. As a result, the warrior must be like nature with its different seasons and provisions to sustain life - always changing and adapting. Samuel, following in the steps of his great-grandfather, would conclude that being a true warrior means knowing when to fight, when to call for peace, when to heal, when to take a stand, when to retreat, and when to use diplomacy. The warrior who can balance such characteristics will, in most cases, maintain the honor of the tribe, as well as sustain its health and existence. He remembers his great-grandfather saying, "Hold tight to the Navajo language. Take care of yourself with your language and wherever you go, you will make a life. There are many things out there that you are not supposed to do. Don't do these things and you will prosper in your life."

The attributes of a warrior were put to the test for Samuel's great-grandfather and the Navajo tribe in 1864 as they endured the brutal journey of the Long Walk from northeastern Arizona and northwestern New Mexico nearly 300 miles southeast to Bosque Redondo. Sam could not comprehend why his people, who by nature were a peaceful tribe, had to leave their homes and be subjected to such horrific living conditions. His great-grandfather was not able to estimate the number of lives lost due to the harsh conditions or the inhumane living conditions on the journey and at Bosque Redondo. He described how those who became too weak or too sick to keep up the pace were left in the wilderness to die, and how the families of the deceased were further insulted because they were not allowed the time to process the loss, nor perform the traditional tribal burial ceremonies. There would be no traditional preparation of the body for burial and no ceremony honoring the deceased's earthly life. For many who died, the place where they fell became their burial location, as their exposed bodies became a part of southwest landscape of cactus and sagebrush. The survivors could only pause momentarily to bid their last respects to their fallen loved one while hoping for the opportunity to return to this very spot to pay proper respect on a future journey home.

Once the weary and sick Navajo Nation arrived at their new home, things did not improve. The conditions in their new "home" called for the warriors of the tribe to lead with the survival skills they had used in battle on the plains, hills and valleys of their homeland. While the U.S. government did provide some shelter and provisions for the tribe, they were inadequate and far from humane. Although some soldiers showed compassion for the captives, many treated them as mere animals, not humans. The white man introduced diseases unknown to the tribe, diseases which had both lethal and life-crippling consequences. The soldiers offered very little medical assistance to combat the illnesses. The young and the elderly took the biggest blows from this new "enemy" which attacked the health of the tribe. The wisdom and knowledge of the medicine men would contribute much to the preservation of the tribe. Their healing methods, including prayers and their formulas of herbs and spices, would help in the recovery of the sick and were attributed with saving many lives. At this point in their history, Samuel's great-grandfather became known as both a wise warrior and a trusted medicine man. While he could not save everyone, many more would have died had it not been for his heroic efforts.

The food in the camp was not nutritious and was much different from their traditional diet of squash, berries, fruits, corn, fish and lamb or goat meat. Sometimes they were able to supplement their meager food supply with a trout from the nearby stream, a wayward bird, or a misfortunate rabbit that wandered within their grasp. Occasionally their captors would provide a cow, but this luxury was rare.

Finally after five long years of captivity, the army decided to sign a treaty and send the Navajo back to their land in the Four Corners area, the region where the states of New Mexico, Arizona, Colorado and Utah meet. Even though the treaty was one-sided (not in their favor), the Navajo people were willing to agree to most anything inorder to be free and to return to the land they loved.

Once again Samuel's great grandfather utilized his skills as a warrior to assist his remaining family and other members of the tribe in making the long journey home. At least this time, the anticipation of returning home would help them find the inner strength and energy to endure the 300-mile journey. Unfortunately, some members of the tribe did not survive the trip, but they died in peace, knowing they were once again a free people and their family members could once again embrace the hope of a future nation. Stories Sam remembers from the sweat lodge told of many hardships faced on the return journey and during the subsequent rebuilding of their homes in their beloved land – stories both unimaginable and difficult to understand for the young boy.

When Samuel was not spending time with his grandfather, he was busy helping with the family's day-to-day work on the ranch or experiencing life as a child in the vast natural playground of the Southwest. For the family to sustain a comfortable existence, each member needed to contribute to the operations of the ranch. During his pre-school years, Samuel was limited in what he could do physically. Nonetheless, he shared in the domestic tasks of the home or watched his father tackle the physically demanding work of running a ranch, which included tending to the livestock and maintaining fences, buildings and other equipment.

This philosophy of life, in a sense, required his family to be one with each other and the tribe. This is not to say there were not disagreements within families and within the tribe, but despite the conflicts and struggles, the determination to do what was best for the family and for the tribe was central to Samuel's upbringing. Whatever challenges life threw at them, the family faced them *together*. Reflecting back in time, Sam indicated that this unity brought comfort to each family member; they understood that they were not facing life on their own. They were taught to take responsibility, both as a member of the family and a member of the of the tribe, and they learned the importance of making decisions in the context of their clan.

One example of the Sandoval's supportive family system occurred during the birth of Samuel's brother. When Sam's mother was in labor, the family loaded up in the wagon and headed to town and the local hospital. Being repeatedly jostled around on the rough and rutted roads did not make for a pleasant ride for a woman in labor. About half way into the five-mile trip to town, the grandmother, graciously taking the role of the midwife, determined that they needed to stop. As Sam recalls, they had no other choice but to stop so his mother could deliver his brother in the open wagon on the dusty, desert road. One minute he was nearly asleep due to the rocking motion of the ride and the next thing he knew, he was awakened by the cries of a newborn. Although there was joy upon the addition of another Navajo boy to the clan, young Samuel feared that the baby's unexpected arrival on the way to town would mean that the family would turn around and return home. However, to his delight, they continued their journey to town so the hospital staff could check to make sure his new brother, Merril, was healthy. Sam readily admits that he was more concerned about missing out on a treat from the local trading post, than he was for his newborn brother.

While some from outside the "Navajo way" might consider his people deprived, Samuel would disagree. His siblings and friends considered their surroundings a vast classroom and playground. Through their daily, intimate experiences with nature, the children acquired the ability to be flexible, adaptable, innovative and creative. The environment was an endless source of education - a natural science lab, a magical art studio and a vast playground. Sam believes the lessons he learned while growing up on the high desert, together with the traditions of the Navajo culture, directly translated into the skills necessary for his successes as a Code Talker and later as a drug and alcohol counselor. Samuel's family was not wealthy by western standards, but they did not know anything different and did not consider themselves poor. Outsiders might have looked at their living conditions and labeled them as impoverished, but they saw themselves as rich in many different ways - primarily in the context of their connection with nature.

There are very few signs remaining today of a working ranch in the place where Samuel grew up. The most prominent structure remaining at his grandmother's place, where he spent a significant amount of time, is the stone chimney, which is over one hundred years old and stands about twelve feet high amongst the sagebrush, cedar, native grasses and cactus. It towers out of the different shades of green, like a miniature-sized stone replica of the massive natural rock structures found in Monument Valley. On a visit to the Four Corners area in preparation for the filming of the documentary, Sam pointed out a few leftover traces of a working ranch: wood posts that had been part of the fenced-in garden and two stable areas. Traces of an abandoned homestead were discovered, including an old kerosene lamp, a sole of a child's shoe and various pieces of brown, green, blue and clear glass found in the location of the dump. Excavations in the area might lead to an assortment of family and domestic artifacts covering several generations. In the distance Samuel pointed out a chimney from a small house where a neighboring family once lived. The structure was abandoned when it became infested with snakes.

As our film crew crossed the dry wash, which at one time was a large river supplying the family with life-giving water on the homestead, our van became stuck in the sand and we were quickly reminded of the unforgiving environment. Fortunately, one member of the crew, our official guide and a man who has spent significant time in the area, had made preparations for such an occurrence by loading extra tire jacks in the van. After an hour and half of hard digging with broken pieces of wood and a shovel borrowed from a nearby oil rig crew, plus additional time taken to scavenge the area for old wood planks to put under the tires, we were able to drive out. During this time-consuming setback, Sam watched with a rare smile on his face and commented, "That was interesting." It must have looked like a comedy skit unfolding before him. Knowing his light-hearted personality, I am certain he chuckled multiple times while sitting in the other vehicle analyzing the scene as we strategized, improvised and finally dug our way out of the sand and sage. The last scene in particular would have given him the most delight. I am confident he was laughing as he watched one of men on our crew, who is large enough to play professional football, charge and made contact with the rear of the van. The jolt he provided proved to be the boost needed to free the vehicle from the sandy terrain.

Nature has taught the Navajo many transferable life lessons. There are seasons and cycles of life that leave clues about what can be expected and how to prepare for it. The changes in nature taught the people to recognize the developmental stages of individuals in the family. Sam's father recognized a change needed to take place in young Samuel's life as a result of some behaviors observed while he and his sister were in charge of the sheep one day. Samuel, who was nearing school age, along with his sister who was a few years younger, were in charge of watching a flock of sheep grazing among the sage in the Checkerboard area. Sam was at the stage in life when his father had to determine whether he would be trained for a ranching career or if he should go to school to learn other skills. The following story was the sign that prompted his father to proceed with this change in direction.

> *My sister and I were out watching the sheep while our father was tending to some other work on the ranch. We decided we would break our boredom from watching the sheep and so we decided to play cars. We went to work creating our vehicles out of mud and using broken glass for the windshields. We were very pleased with the variety of cars and pickups with their brown, green and clear windows in our collection. In fact we were so engaged with our play that we were startled when our father came upon us and asked, "Where are the sheep?" We, of course, had no idea; it was at that moment my father decided it was time for me to go to school to obtain more discipline. Shortly*

after that event, he enrolled my brother and I in the Navajo Methodist Mission School in Farmington, NM.

Lessons Learned

Samuel's favorite Bible verses: Psalm 91:1-2 (King James Bible)

*He that dwelleth in the secret place of the most High shall abide under the shadow of the Almighty.
I will say of the Lord, He is my refuge and my fortress: my God; in Him will I trust.*

Quite often in interviews and talks, Samuel shares how he wishes he had paid more attention to his great-grandfather's stories in the smoke-filled sweat lodge. He is only able to recall a few of the hundreds of powerful stories, stories that could easily have filled the pages of a lengthy book. Sam speaks of the great wisdom and insightful advice his great-grandfather attempted to pass along to his sleepy-eyed grandson. He tells of his honor and bravery, and of his respect for the tribal history, heritage, language and culture. His great-grandfather taught him that hard work and hard play, plus deep Navajo spiritual enlightenment, would serve him and his family well and lead to a life of contentment and peace. Sam's deep convictions and passion to do what he can do to sustain the richness of the culture, history and language for generations of Navajos to come stems from these times as a child. He often tells others that his goal is to outlive his great-grandfather, and he hopes that with the time afforded him, he will be able to inspire others to embrace and carry on the Navajo way.

Reflections

As I reflect on many interviews with the Sandoval's through the lens of my counseling background, I am fascinated by their contentment and calm outlook on life. They conveyed details about intense events and memories that would cause me anxiety and apprehension, with a deeply rooted calm; these were normal life happenings on the reservation. After spending many hours with Samuel and Malula, both in the artificial setting of the studio and the natural setting of their home in the Shiprock, New Mexico area, it became apparent that their serene approach to life, family, tribe, nature, and culture is genuine and admirable. In story after story, the theme of the acceptance of life as it comes was constant. Though Samuel did not display the emotions one might expect when telling some of his life stories, it does not mean he is not passionate about the content of the accounts. His passion is evident in his actions and his words. No doubt some of the translation of that passion was lost or hard to recognize due to ignorance about the Navajo language and culture by this white guy from Kansas.

Family/Clan is very important and sacred to the Navajo and it is important to pay tribute to them by listing them below:

Maternal Great-Grandfather – Hostien Cly (Left Handed Man) DOB: Unknown
Clan: Ta'neezah'nii (Tangle Clan)

Maternal Great-Grandmother, wife of Hostien Cly
Navajo Only – As'sned'des'pah (Lady Going to War) DOB: Unknown
Clan: Naashi'ezhi'dine'e (Zuni Clan)

Father – Julian Sandoval, Jr. (1895-1952)

Mother – Helen S. Sandoval (1900-1930)
Clan: Naashi'ezhi'dine'e (Zuni Clan)

Brothers:
Robert H. Sandoval (May 15, 1918-1940)
William Sandoval DOB: Unknown
Samuel F. Sandoval (Born October 24, 1923)
Merril L. Sandoval (April 18, 1928- February 15, 2008
Rodger H. Sandoval (August 1928-January 13, 2003)

Sister:
Beulah S. Kelly (May 1932-January 12, 2004)

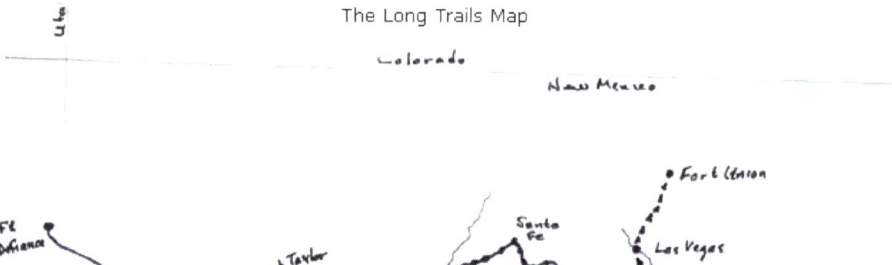

Sketch of The Long Walk taken from Sam's Scrapbook

Just below the horizon is the area of Samuel's childhood home and the sweat lodge. (JCCC photo)

The old stone chimney from Sam's grandmother's homestead. (JCCC photo)

Samuel pictured with his father, brothers and sister. (Family photo, circa, 1939)

21

Corral area of Grandmother's homestead. (JCCC photo)

Remnants of Grandmother's homestead. (JCCC photo)

Another remnant from Grandmother's homestead. (JCCC photo)

Mesa area where Sam would have grazed sheep as a youth. (JCCC photo)

Typical grazing area near Turtle Mountain. (JCCC photo)

Chapter Two

School

One of Samuels's favorite hymns: *Jesus is Mine*

We were glad to be home from our school in Farmington for Christmas break and were on our way to church, as we were most every Sunday. My father and mother were in the front seat of our car, while the rest of us were half asleep in the back seat. Father usually had the radio on in the car when we traveled and did his best to find a station that would come in clearly. We were not far from home when suddenly the regular programming was interrupted by the announcement that the Japanese Empire had just bombed Pearl Harbor. Father quickly stopped the car. Some of us peeked over the back seat, while others climbed over and crowded together in the front. With our parents, we listened intently to the details of the attack and were mesmerized by the news. Without warning, my brother jumped out of the car and starting running towards home. As he left the car, he yelled something about needing to go back and tell Grandmother the news. Later he told us that when he arrived home out of breath and told our grandmother about the attack, she paused with a confused look on her face and commented, "Why would the lady at the restaurant in town bomb Pearl Harbor?" You see, that elderly lady who owned the restaurant in town was the only oriental person our grandmother knew. (Samuel's first memory of hearing of the bombing of Pearl Harbor.)

While the track record of many missionary schools has been questioned and there have been allegations and realities concerning of the cruel treatment of Native Americans, this was not the experience Sam had at the Navajo Methodist Mission School (NMMS) in Farmington, New Mexico. He describes his time at the boarding school as instrumental to his physical, mental and spiritual development and maturity. As he puts it, "This is where I learned more of the *do's and do not's* needed for life." Despite the school's discouragement of some Navajo cultural practices and its restriction against speaking the Navajo language on the school grounds, Samuel benefited greatly from his time at the school during his formative years. He described his years at the school by saying, "They were very kind to me."

His overall reflections of his time at NMMS are positive, but there were rules that were questionable and unnecessary from his viewpoint. In fact, had the future Code Talkers who attended this school obeyed all the rules, it might have greatly crippled the effectiveness of the code and its contribution to the war. One example of blatant disregard of the NMMS rules began early in his schooling. Sam did not know any English before starting school. Before taking him to school, his father explained the rules to him. One of these rules was that students were forbidden to speak Navajo while on school property.

Fortunately, most of the students at NMMS ignored this rule. They spoke only English in the presence of the school staff, but spoke Navajo amongst themselves. Sam recalls communicating in his native language in the corners of the playground, in the dorm, and in his bunk at night.

It does not take a genius to deduce that mastery of language is a vital ingredient for any linguistic code development. In this case, the Navajo language had no alphabet and no written text, which meant the spoken word was its foundation. Though some see the lack of a written language as problematic, there were unintentional benefits that resulted from their reliance on verbal communication. The Navajo developed a capacity to remember and retain information through day-to-day conversations and the countless hours of storytelling. They relied on their memories rather than referencing back to a written document. Sam's ability to remember large amounts of information began at early age in the sweat lodge listening to his grandfather and was further cultivated at boarding school. These memory skills provided a vital foundation as he learned more about language and communication.

The philosophy of education at the school was reflected in the day-to-day schedule of the students through a balance of academic and vocational learning. Embedded within the curriculum were the guiding principles of faith, discipline, respect and good old' hard work. Parents appreciated the balance in the curriculum. If there were any objections, it was often the result of teachings that came into direct conflict with Navajo ways, often due to the ignorance of the white man in understanding the Navajo culture. Had the educators taken the time to truly understand the Navajo way of life, the cultural infusion could have enriched the learning experience and enhanced the academic content. As Sam put it, "That what you don't understand or don't try to understand, you will probably fear." At times, the foundational Christian teachings and the Navajo religious teachings did not line up to everyone's satisfaction and interpretation. For Sam, there were more similarities than differences; he embraced both the Christian faith and the "Navajo way" and stayed true to both.

A typical school day began early with assigned chores for all students. Chores, which started at 5:00 AM, included making beds, helping in the kitchen, laundry duty, and feeding the small collection of horses, cows, sheep, pigs and chickens. Eggs needed gathered and cows needed milked. The academic day included the traditional subjects of mathematics, language arts (English), and reading. Other subjects of study included the Christian faith, sciences, geography and history. Music, drama, art and physical education were also a part of their education. Their day concluded with recreation, dinner and a mandatory study hall at 7:00 PM. The study hall time was instrumental to academic success and also became a monitored social time where ideas were shared and individual tutoring was provided as needed.

Sam recalls butchering a sheep or pig twice a month and fondly recalls the fresh foods they ate. He often volunteered to take the leftovers to feed to the pigs after meals because it meant he would be rewarded with a fresh slice of bread from the girls working in the kitchen. Both girls and boys helped with the apple picking and the making of apple cider, the favorite drink of the students. One of the other favorite treats was to take an apple, drill a good-sized hole in the middle where the core resided, and then replace the hollowed out area with ice cream. In the winter, the apples were set outside to freeze, which resulted in an ice cream apple delight. Other chores included the cutting and storage of the hay, chopping and gathering wood to feed the boilers which heated the school, and traveling to the local coal mine to get their share of coal which was also used in the boilers.

Vocational education included the teaching of traditional domestic skills for the females and the trade skills for the males. The domestic skills taught typically aligned with the traditional female roles of the time period and included things learned in a Navajo home, such as weaving and baking. In this culture and time period, the female was expected to be able to perform homemaking duties such as cooking, mending, and taking care of the children, for example. As the girls grew older, they were expected to help more with the livestock and gardening responsibilities.

Vocational education for male students was composed of things that might be taught at a trade school. They learned carpentry, basic construction, the butchering process, livestock management, and masonry. The complete masonry process was taught beginning with the selection and transportation of the bright red clay from local riverbanks. The boys learned the best mixture needed to make bricks and how to use horses to move the large outdoor circular mixing apparatus. They learned to build the wood molds, how to pour in the clay mixture, the methods for properly drying the bricks and finally the kiln process. Remnants of the brick-making operation are still visible on campus as some of the bricks made by the students were used in building the campus church, which is still in use today.

Carpentry was another skill taught at the school. Sam noted that they didn't use modern-day machinery, but learned to use a chisel and a hammer. Their carpentry skills were used in the building of the chapel. Dark-stained beams with hand-carved ornate designs outline the stucco walls and the wood ceiling. The handcrafted pews, altars and pulpit with traditional Southwest designs carved into them are unique. The stained glass windows light up the interior of the chapel like bright sunbeams shining through thousands of twirling diamonds, filling the chapel with a rainbow of colors. Samuel and other NMMS students are responsible for much of the construction and embellishment of the chapel. It's hard to imagine that those young students had the ability to create such architectural beauty. Sam commented several times how very fortunate they were to have had learned such valuable skills at such an early age.

The school was based on a holistic approach to education. Beyond academics, administrators felt it was important to teach the students how to interact with each other socially. They taught the proper social boundaries and etiquette between males and females. Strict rules were in place dictating where and when males and females could associate with each other. They were closely monitored while in class, and during meals and recreational activities. Males and females had separate living areas on campus. Any social activities that included both males and females required chaperones. Proper respect and manners between a male and female in public and private settings were taught and modeled.

> *Little did I know at the time that even our recreational activities at the school would prepare me to one day be a warrior. I am confident that some of the strategies and skills attained during our time on the playground helped me survive the battlefields during my South Pacific tour of duty. If someone from the outside were to observe a particular game we played with regularity, which required the use of wild horses in the area, they would have certainly labeled it as dangerous and threatening to the health and welfare of children. This game would certainly not be permitted today as a sanctioned recreational activity for children, or adults for that matter. (One of Samuel's memories from his school days.)*

Recreation, from the traditional competitive sports of baseball and basketball, to the less structured activities of kickball, stickball and foot racing, was a cherished experience for many of the students. One of the more popular recreational activities, referenced in the memory above, was wild horse tag. The male students were typically the only participants, but occasionally a female student was brave enough to join in the fun. Spectators expressed their amusement of the activity through laughter or the shaking of their heads, depending on the outcome of the activity. Bands of wild horses commonly roamed in this part of the high desert. The horses usually minded their own business if their human counterparts allowed them to. The imaginations and pent up energy of the young students combined with the untamed, spooky nature of the wild horses, were the perfect recipe for trouble. The game began with the boys digging small foxholes in the open area on the bluff behind the school. The goal of the game was to irritate the horses enough so they would give chase. When a cooperative horse began to chase the boys, they would quickly race the opposite direction and dive into the prepared foxholes, hopefully prior to being tagged by a horse. The student who was able to dive into a foxhole before being butted or trampled by a horse was the winner. Of course, being caught by an irritable, angry horse was risky, but fortunately, no one was seriously injured. The brave warriors laughed all day about their victories and their near misses. Sam often lay in his bed at night replaying in his mind the matador-like experiences. He got the sense that the horses actually enjoyed the game as much as the boys. Later, while lying in his Marine bunk, exhausted after a major battle, Samuel remembers how his mind would drift back to those days of wild horse tag and how that game with the horses had helped prepare him for the more serious game of running and jumping into the nearest foxhole or bomb crater during battle.

Another out-of-the-ordinary activity was the tire race. While a deep layer of snow was preferred for this competition because it greatly reduced the number of bumps and bruises obtained, the children tended to ignore how much snow was actually on the ground. Students gathered old truck tires in the area and rolled them to the top of the bluff behind the school. One by one, each student would then tuck his or her body into the center of the tire while others held the tire in place. Once the participant was ready, the tire was pushed down the steep hill. When there was plenty of snow, the ride resulted in smiles and laughter. But those times when snow was lacking, the ride resulted in pained expressions as they landed on the hard ground. Those who made it to the bottom without mishap enjoyed watching the others trying to regain their balance after their ride. At the conclusion of this game, riders tolerated the inevitable scrapes and bruises with pride, like a badge of honor.

Because of the distance the Sandoval home was from the school, it was impractical for the family to visit or for the children to travel to home except during Thanksgiving and Christmas breaks. The Sandoval family was close-knit, and Sam found it difficult to go months at a time without seeing his family and being in the familiar surroundings of his home. Occasionally, his family would travel to the school if Sam or one of his siblings was involved in a special program. Knowing the sacrifice it took to make the trip, he and his siblings were very appreciative when the family would come for a visit. The children returned home each summer to work on the ranch. It was often a struggle to return to the school, especially during the early years of his education. Eventually, he and his siblings became used to the boarding school routine and, during their high school years, began to look forward to returning to school.

FMMS not only had significant impact on Samuel's physical and intellectual development, but his spiritual growth also flourished during his time there. The foundation for his Christian walk was laid in the classrooms and chapel services and it was here that he accepted Jesus Christ as his Lord and Savior. Though not all Native Americans had a favorable experience with Christian missionaries, his encounters were very positive. He soon discovered a way to embrace Christianity while still maintaining a deep respect and appreciation for the Navajo traditions. While he admits he does not understand all the mysteries of the Christian life or those of the Navajo way, he has seen God work in mysterious ways on both military and domestic battlefields. Sam freely shares how his knowledge and trust in the person of Christ has been instrumental in his ability to persevere and overcome struggles he faced during the war and after he returned home.

An unexpected accident during Samuel's senior year left emotional and physical scars, but also taught him how to endure pain and persevere through adversity. The older students enjoyed cookouts on the school property. At one of these cookouts, Sam wandered too close to the flames and his pant leg caught on fire. Immediately he and others nearby frantically tried to dowse the fire. At first Sam did not think the burn was something to be concerned about, but as he recovered from the shock of it all, the ensuing pain led him to seek medical attention. He had sustained third degree burns on a small area of his leg. If recovery had transpired as planned, this may not have become a major ordeal, but the tissue on Sam's leg was not responding to the treatments or the grafting process. Days in the hospital turned into weeks, and the weeks turned into six months. Sam hadn't expected to miss much school and knew he could easily catch up on the work, but as time went on he began to wonder if he would need to drop out of his senior year. If not for the encouragement of the faculty and his schoolmates, he might have done just that, but this team of supporters proceeded to implement a plan to help him to keep up with his studies. His leg slowly began to respond to the treatments and he was able to return to school with a few months left in his senior year. He was extremely thankful and moved by the extra tutoring and other support he received from his teachers and classmates.

The lessons these Navajo students learned while at NMMS during their school years greatly benefited them after high school as they entered the work force or prepared for college. Communication and teamwork were valuable lessons they mastered as they worked alongside each another. Sam is convinced that the training he received was instrumental to the success of the Code Talkers as they served as soldiers and their mastery of the English language, both written and spoken, was key to their success in developing a very complex code. Their exposure to the "white man's world," including its history and culture, was also instrumental in designing a code described as not only efficient, but tactically effective and brilliant. These Navajo adolescents, who had limited exposure to the world outside the reservation or school and to the cultural and social norms outside the Southwest, were able to make an extraordinary contribution to the war effort.

As Sam reflected on his education, he thought it was ironic that a native people surrounded by vast deserts would someday be trying to free a native people whose land was surrounded by vast oceans, a people enslaved, starved, misused, abused, humiliated and killed by invaders of their lands. He would represent and fight for a government who once committed similar atrocities against the Native Americans in this country. In many ways, the Navajo Code Talkers had something in common with those who they were trying to liberate from the clutches of the Japanese. Sam had an idea, from the stories he heard from his great-grandfather, what it must feel like to have a people take your land, imprison you and treat you as a second-class citizen or even something less. For Sam, this was more than a fight for an unknown people, but rather a struggle to liberate another native people who he could empathize with - a people he had more in common with than one might expect.

Sam graduated from the Navajo Methodist Mission School in 1942 and was faced with making a decision about what to do after graduation. Work was hard to find with the war still going strong in Europe, so his choices were limited. He did attempt to join the military, but since he was not considered a U.S. citizen he could not serve. He was willing to serve his country, but was considered a foreigner – even though his people were living here before the Europeans even knew North America existed. However, it is interesting how the government sees things differently when it needs something. One hot summer day in Farmington, a Marine recruiter stopped him out of the blue and asked him if he was Navajo and if he was fluent in the language. Samuel was suspicious, but reluctantly admitted that he was Navajo and that he knew the language. The recruiter then asked if he knew any other Navajo men his age. He again hesitated, but acknowledged that he did. The sergeant seemed very interested and began to explain that Uncle Sam needed them. With urgency, he asked Sam to round up as many of his friends as possible and to meet him at the recruitment office a few blocks away.

A few weeks later Samuel, along with seven other Navajo young men and the principal from their school in Farmington, found themselves standing on the porch of the administrative building posing for a group photo before boarding a bus to Camp Pendleton in California. As they stood on the school grounds, the crowd of family members, former classmates, current students, faculty and community members who gathered to wish them blessings and to honor their bravery astonished them. Many years later, a former classmate shared with Sam her vivid memories of that day. She remembered the young girls either crying or embracing one another, while the future Navajo Code Talkers proudly stood with their chests puffed out. Others were cheering and congratulating the boys, or singing songs honoring their courage and dedication to America and the Navajo Nation. Family members in attendance that day were both apprehensive and proud of their young sons going to war. Most of these young men had never left the Southwest, experienced the complexities and chaos of a large city, seen an ocean, or lived in an environment that was predominately Caucasian. They were not only concerned for their safe return, but also wondered what changes would they see in the innocent, young men when they returned home. The parents were familiar with stories of men who had returned from the war as shells of their former selves. They were aware of the casualty rates and how the U.S was suffering many defeats in the Pacific conflict. Despite their legitimate concerns and the fact that the relationship between the Navajo Nation and the U.S. had a blemished past, there was still a great pride in what these boys were doing to honor both nations.

Lessons Learned

Because of his personal educational experience and the opportunities it provided for him, Samuel strongly believes in the value of education. After the war, he obtained both bachelor's and a master's degrees. While he understands that a traditional four year college degree is not for everyone, he is convinced that some level of training after high school is vitally important to long term livelihood and health for individuals and communities. Following the war, as he gave talks to K-12 students and their parents, Samuel continually emphasized the importance of education for the health and welfare of their families and Navajo Nation as a whole. He is especially concerned that the Navajo language and culture is not being taught with the same importance as it once was, which causes him to wonder if it will be lost in future generations. Losing the language, equal in Samuel's mind to losing the culture, would be tragic and would threaten the existence of the Navajo way of life. The Navajo language was not only essential for defeating the "enemy," but continues to be the heart and soul of the culture.

Reflections

While touring the Navajo Methodist Mission School with Samuel, it was evident that reliving the memories of his school days energized him. He was clearly proud of his school and the classmates with whom he shared the majority of his developmental years. His eyes lit up and his voice reflected excitement as he shared memory after memory of learning, working and playing in that place. He proudly led us into the chapel and pointed out the beautiful architectural details and the hand-carved woodwork contributed by him and his classmates. The recollections were as fresh in his mind as though they took place just recently instead of decades ago.

Sam, 6th grade. (Family photo)

Navajo Methodist Mission School (NMMS) overlooking the area the students played the wild horse game and near the area where they launched their tires in the winter. (Photo NMMS archives)

Photo of Navajo boys playing at the FMMS. (Photo from the school's archives)

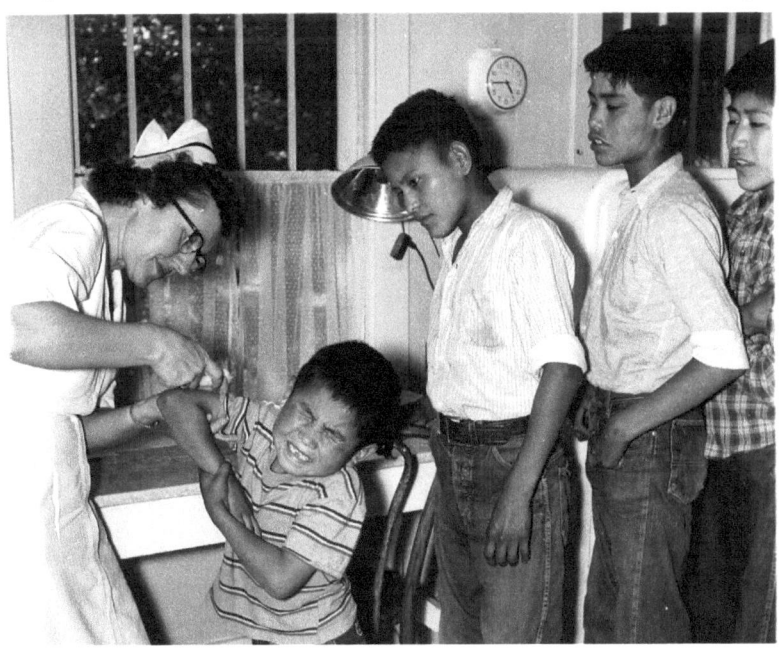

Photo of students waiting their turn for a vaccination from the school nurse (Photo from the school's archives)

(A collection of photos from the school archives)

A recent photo of the classroom and faculty building. (JCCC photo)

Sam in front of the ornate doors of the chapel. (JCCC photo)

A view of the front of the chapel. (JCCC photo)

A chair in the chapel. (JCCC photo)

Samuel on the porch of the Administration Building where he gathered with the group before leaving for California in 1943. (JCCC photo)

From Left to Right: Robert Yazzie, Albert Henry, David Tsosie, Samuel F. Sandoval, Chee Martin, Francis Bates, Carl Todacheenie, George Soce, Dr. Brooks, Wilfred Billey, James Nahkai, Frank Harris. (Photo from Samuel's Code Talker Scrapbook)

Chapter Three

Dine' Bazaad Yee Atah Naaye'e' Yik'eh Deesdlii

The Navajo Language was used to Defeat the Enemy!

As the drill sergeant handed me my M1 rifle, an overwhelming fear came over me. I knew it was not the fear of handling a rifle; from a young age on the reservation, I had handled weapons. As I stood there staring at the barrel of the rifle, I became more anxious and nervous. I began to get hot and to perspire. Suddenly a thought came to my mind. Years ago my grandfather talked about the Treaty of 1868. One of the articles in the treaty emphatically stated that the Navajo people would no longer bear arms. I began to think to myself, "Is this a trick? Would I be punished or imprisoned for bearing arms?"

Our confidence and bravery were a bit shaken as we tried to get our bearings in the newness of our surroundings. The language and nuances of the military culture were a bit overwhelming causing us to instinctively stick close together. The military encouraged us to become close as a unit; they did not discourage us from keeping to ourselves or from refraining from intermingling with the other non-native soldiers. While we would learn to work alongside our fellow soldiers, the military made it very clear that we were to be left to ourselves and that we were to be regarded with respect as fully invested warriors. Over time through weeks and months of training and fighting alongside one another in battle, we earned respect from our comrades. (Recollections of Samuel Sandoval)

Brief Service Timeline:

- March 26, 1943 - Physical exam for USMC. 60 Navajo boys passed their physical.
- April 4, 1943 - Basic training at San Diego Station, San Diego, California.
- June 9, 1943 - Completion of basic training. Moved on to advanced training at Camp Pendleton, Oceanside, California. New recruits' duties included the expansion of the Navajo Code. The first group of 29 had only 200 words. The new recruits contributed 600 more words and had to have them memorized for combat duties.
- July 20, 1943 - Training completed.
- September 8, 1943 - Moved out to sea for actual combat duties.
- September 21, 1943 - At a staging area Noanai, New Caledonia. Disbursed into three different divisions. Five of us went to the 1st Marine Division, Guadalcanal war zone.
- Samuel participated in five campaigns:
  - Guadalcanal, 1943
  - Bougainville, 1943
  - Guam, 1944
  - Peleliu, 1944

- Okinawa, 1945
- December 27, 1945 Sailed from China to USA.
- January 12, 1946 - Arrived at San Diego, California.
- January 1946 – Honorable Discharge.

Inside the bus was a group of green young men who knew nothing of military life and a predominately white military culture. Soon these new recruits were processed, sorted and assigned. All of the Code Talkers served in the 1st Marine Division and Samuel was assigned to Platoon 297.

The routine for the new recruits included the normal basic training required for all soldiers, plus specialized military training in communications. On top of the physical and emotional rigors of basic training, the schedule also included time for the development and learning of the code. Fortunately for the Navajo recruits, the physical training was not too overwhelming as life on the reservation had conditioned their bodies well for the demands they faced. In fact, their drill sergeant became very agitated one day by what appeared to be a lackadaisical approach to training. After a long run, the sergeant stopped for a few minutes to let the troops catch their breath and to drill more Marine propaganda into their heads. Though the non-Navajo troops were on their knees, struggling to regain their breath, three Navajos were standing in a relaxed, casual posture with their hands in their pockets, a common stance for them, intently and respectfully listening to every word their leader had to say. To him, their posture screamed an attitude that implied, "Is that all you've got for us? You can't break us!" The sergeant quickly ordered the young men to run to the beach and stuff their pockets with sand – all of the pockets in both their pants and shirts. Once their pockets were full of sand, they were ordered to sew the pockets closed. After two weeks of this added burden, which hardly seemed to faze the Navajos, the sergeant conceded that these young men were in excellent physical shape and as tough as nails emotionally. He discovered they had outstanding marksmanship skills and were quick learners when exposed to weapons they had never seen. Many were able to quickly adapt to the hand-to-hand techniques preferred by the Marine handbook and they also enjoyed showing off some of their own moves from hours of wrestling with each other at school. The obstacle course was actually fun and reminded them of dodging the wild horses on the school grounds.

The military allowed the men little time to become comfortable in their new surroundings before connecting the new Navajo recruits with the original 29 Navajo soldiers who were already hard at work developing the code. As part of the orientation for the new recruits, it was explained that the military had high expectations that this code would be the ingenious weapon that would turn the tide of the war. The original 29 Code Talkers had already created approximately 200 words of the vocabulary and they immediately began to teach them to the new recruits. The new recruits were quick to catch on to the code. After a number of days of intense study and practice of the first 200 words, the group realized they would need, at minimum, to double the number of words. The group, now consisting of 80 Code Talkers expanded the code to 800 words before they were deployed into action in the Pacific. Sam was a part of this original group of 80 men credited with the development of the Navajo Code, which would be used in live battle operations.

Once a portion of the code was developed, it needed to be tested against the standard communication of the day, Morris Code, before more time was allotted for the completion of the new code. Using the standard Morris Code took an average of 20 minutes from its delivery to the point of the order being carried out. Because of the amount of time it took, it was vulnerable to being intercepted by the enemy before action was taken on the battlefield. In fact, it was getting so bad it seemed the enemy had a direct line of communication that told them every move the U.S. military was planning to make. To experiment, two teams of communication specialists were given a message to send – one team used the current form of communication (Morris Code) and the other team used the newly developed Navajo Code. It took the team who used Morris Code over an half hour to send, verify and execute the message. It took the team using the Navajo Code only 30 seconds to do the same. The Navajo code had to pass three measures to be considered successful: accuracy, security and speed. The code passed all three with flying colors. The officers did not need any prodding to request the necessary resources to finish the development of the code and make it operational. They felt a sense of urgency knowing that their offering towards the war effort had the potential to save precious lives on the battlefield. Because the Navajo language had no written alphabet and therefore no written language, they were confident no one would be able to break the code, at least until after the war.

It was vital that the communication could be easily delivered and interpreted in the middle of a heated operation. As their military vocabulary increased, they realized that they would need to create more military words because the Navajo language had few words associated with the military. Words were required to communicate about weaponry, communications equipment, military protocol, and rank. Most of the code words they invented were associated with their culture and what was familiar to them from their childhood on the reservation. It seemed natural that the words would correspond to nature, or to Navajo traditions, or to things from their everyday lives. After all, no one was more knowledgeable about these things than they were. For example, the Navajo language had no word for *tank*, so they used the word *turtle* (hard shell, slow moving). They had no word for *submarine*, so they chose to use the word they had made up for *shark*. After arriving at Bougainville where they saw their first action, they noticed the *Zero*, a Japanese plane, sounded like a washing machine. *Washing machine* became the code word for the *Zero*! As they continued their project to develop the code during basic training, the soldiers had little comprehension of the kinds of words they would need. By the time the soldiers found themselves in action, they realized they required words for things they hadn't even known existed, such as new types of weaponry and battle tactics, different kinds of terrain, and cultural nuances from island to island. These words were not on their linguistic radar back at

Camp Pendleton. For example, they had coined only one word for people of the Orient. This became problematic since the Japanese were the enemy, but the Chinese and other island people were, for the most part, allies. They noticed that the Chinese had long braided ponytails in many photographs, so the Navajo word meaning *braided hair* was used to reference their allies with oriental features. Sam even recalls the necessity of adding new words while in the thick of battle.

Sixty-two letters were created in this alphabet - mainly for redundancy, another attempt to confuse the enemy. In some instances, they had the choice of using three different words that meant the same thing to perplex the enemy. For example, a Code Talker might need to send a message that had the word *tank* in it. To indicate the letter *t,* the Code Talker could use the word *tea*, *tooth* or *turkey* to represent the letter *t.* The Code Talker would have three different words he could choose from for each corresponding letter in the word *tank*. In the Navajo dialect, it is very difficult to differentiate between different words, so even if the enemy could understand the Navajo dialect, they became bewildered when they could not distinguish any consistent pattern. The Code Talkers, if necessary, also had the latitude to use words to qualify the nature of the tank. They could use the Navajo word for *fire* to describe the tank with a flamethrower on board. The flexibility to use the Navajo language, within the structured linguistic foundation of the code added even more confusion for those trying desperately to break the code. By the end of the war, the code consisted of well over 800 words, not counting the other words they used as needed from the Navajo language.

Sam tells the story of an observation plane circling the island as he and his comrades were pinned down on the beach at Guam. The radio operator in the plane happened to be a Navajo; however, he did not know the code. The flight captain heard the communication between the Code Talkers on the beach and asked the Navajo soldier in the plane to interpret. After a few minutes, the radio operator reported to the captain in a confused tone of voice, "Sir, the best I can make out is that they are having breakfast on the beach with eggs." He was right about them being on the beach, but no one was eating while the battle was raging all around them. *Beach* meant something completely different in the code and *eggs* was a code word for bombs.

Sam's wife, Malula, who speaks fluent Navajo, has been the unofficial archivist and roving records-keeper of the Code Talkers for years. She has spent hours listening to the Code Talkers converse in code during their gatherings, but is still unable to make any sense of what she is hearing. She describes their communication as "gibberish." While she is able to understand many of the words, they make no sense in the context and sequence in which they are spoken.

Another unique aspect of the Code Talker story is the assignment of a bodyguard to each Code Talker. The purpose of the bodyguard was two-fold: to protect the Code Talker and to protect the code. Most combat soldiers were assigned a rifle or an automatic weapon, while officers in the field were also issued a side arm. However, the bodyguards for the Code Talkers were issued a standard Colt 1911 for close contact fighting and also to kill the very Code Talker they were ordered to protect (as a last resort) if the Navajo was in jeopardy of being captured by the enemy. Fortunately, for the Navajo Code Talkers and their bodyguards, no Code Talker was ever in danger of being captured. Interestingly, according to conversations Sam had with other Code Talkers over the years, some of the Navajo soldiers were aware of the mission of the bodyguards, but many were confused about their role or had no grasp of the scope of their task. In Sam's case, he finally was made aware of the role and purpose of his bodyguard when he was in China following the surrender of Japan. When asked about his experience with his bodyguard, he seemed puzzled that the officer referred to him as a "bodyguard." After his commanding officer explained to Sam the role of his comrade, who had been by his side during many difficult battles and experiences, Sam paused and replied, "He never pulled out his .45 and I am still alive, so I must have done ok." The officer chuckled and agreed he did a fine job. During battle, Sam remembered thinking how strange it was that this soldier always seemed to be nearby, but it all made sense after his visit with the commanding officer.

Approximately 145 of the over 400 combat-ready Navajo Code Talkers saw action. Since no one knew how long the war would last, military officials prepared 800 Navajos who could be activated if necessary. Of those who saw action, 13 were killed and none were declared missing in action or captured (officially). It is remarkable, given the number of island invasions the Code Talkers participated in and the fact that they were designated to advance in the first wave, that only 13 were killed. All of these men who saw action contributed to the development of words during the war as needed, although many of the war-time words were not added to the official *Code Talker Dictionary*.

There is one story of the "unofficial" capture of a Code Talker. To understand this humorous tale, the reader needs to understand the "perfect storm" of war. The common soldier is placed in an environment with hundreds of other adolescents whose brains are still developing (especially the frontal lobe which impacts judgment). This causes them to act impulsively, take risks and become enamored with shiny objects. Military officials know their young troops are vulnerable to temptation – especially during the down time between battles. Soldiers are often tempted to confiscate war paraphernalia including guns, knives, uniforms, or helmets – the shinier the object is, the better. Though there are dangerous repercussions, it was tempting to stash it away or mail it home. (In fact, Sam boxed up a Japanese rifle, put his home address on the box and shipped it home. He would still have it if not for a relative finding it and selling it.) The military was not as concerned with the men keeping the items as much as it was with the risks taken to collect these war trophies. The Japanese also took note of this pilfering as they observed their own soldiers, as well as the behavior of U.S. troops. The enemy decided to turn these "treasures" into deadly booby traps, knowing treasure seekers would take the bait. Army soldiers were the most susceptible treasure hunters since they were assigned the role of cleanup after the Marines had secured the area. In this case on Guadalcanal, the U.S. Army was in the process of rounding up prisoners. One prisoner, who claimed to be a Marine and a Code Talker, perplexed them. After interrogation, which included being stripped of his clothes, they called up some Code Talkers who were in the rear sector. Sam was among this group who arrived to find a naked, dejected soldier who had been mistaken as Japanese by the Caucasian soldiers who had had limited exposure to Native Americans. The Navajo soldier was elated to see familiar faces and it took only a brief exchange of words between the Code Talkers and the Army soldiers before they were satisfied that the story checked out. Needless to say, the treasure hunter learned a valuable lesson about being in the wrong place at the wrong time in his hunt for treasures and he took a lot of ribbing about his adventure.

The top brass were anxious to put their secret weapon, the Navajo Code, into action. The U.S needed some strategic wins on the Pacific Front, not because of lack of effort or ability on the part of the U.S. troops, but because the enemy seemed to know in advance what their every move would be on the battlefield. Thankfully, the Code Talkers had extra time to practice the code and their radio operation skills on their long trip over the Pacific and during the ensuing field orientation and training at their new base camp.

Guadalcanal

Sam's first invasion experience was in Guadalcanal in November of 1943. They were only there for a brief time before leaving for the Bougainville campaign. While two main battles on Guadalcanal were in the mop up stages, there were Japanese holdouts, who either wanted to continue to fight or did not receive the news of retreat. They had short time on Guadalcanal to refine their skills in an actual war setting. This became their exposure to war as they saw the devastation left behind from the battles and counter battles that occurred on Guadalcanal. This period of patrolling and additional communications training further prepared the soldier for the next battle, although no amount of training can fully prepare a soldier for the reality of battle.

Not only did the Code Talkers participate in the first wave of action, they were usually on or near the front lines in order to have the best visual advantage for accurate communication. They also participated in reconnaissance missions and on patrol, both high-risk ventures. While on one memorable reconnaissance mission, Sam became frustrated with the physical awkwardness of his Marine bodyguard, who had already given away his position to the enemy on a previous occasion. In Samuel's words, "I was not very fond of unnecessarily being shot at." This time was no different and his fellow Marine from Brooklyn needed reassigned or Sam was bound to have a "bullet with his name on it." After returning to headquarters, Sam went straight to his sergeant and told him that his bodyguard was a nice enough fellow, but he needed a replacement bodyguard or he would not go out again. His superior knew the Navajo soldier well enough to know that if he complained, it was more than likely a reality and a serious issue. The next day Sam was assigned a new bodyguard.

Bougainville

Sam's second action came in November of 1943 at Bougainville. The initial invasion could not be described as uneventful, but was relatively smooth, especially compared to later invasions at Peleliu, Guam and Okinawa. There are rare moments in war, during unforeseen situations, where humor could be found. In fact, if not for the occasional humorous encounter that served to provide some mental relief, more soldiers would have been emotionally incapacitated. While his unit was in a temporary stalemate near the beachhead, Sam and another Code Talker were manning a Browning Automatic Rifle (BAR). When there is a lull in the action and soldiers have let their guards down, it is especially important to be on the lookout for another, unexpected barrage of fighting from the enemy or a sneak attack. Knowing this, the troops were unusually anxious and trigger-happy. Suddenly, in a location where no U.S. soldiers were expected to be, some bushes started to move! Immediately, the Code Talker opened up with his BAR in the direction of the movement. This caused a chain reaction of others firing on the same location. After riddling the area with relentless gunfire, one of the officers stopped the gunfire. Shortly after the ceasefire was called, a herd of wild pigs came running out of the bushes. The Code Talker who initiated the shooting laughingly accepted his new nickname of "Porky."

The ensuing battles on the island were not humorous as Sam came face-to-face with his own mortality. After numerous skirmishes and what seemed like full-blown jungle warfare, the soldiers were once again on the march. They marched in two lines on the shoulders of the road, fatigued and miserable due to the fighting and the heat. Sam recalls being in a marching trance. Had it not been for the horrible conditions, he could have almost fallen asleep as his body instinctively responded to the rhythmic march they were on. Then, out of nowhere, the high-pitched whine of a Japanese *Zero* broke through the trance and dance of the march and his body automatically dove for cover. As bullets pounded the ground leaving ten-inch divots in the road, he felt the sting of shattered seashells and pebbles hit the side of his body from head to toe. Luckily, the pilot only took one pass at them and then left. Immediately, the horrific screams of pain and smells of death were in the air. Calls for medics echoed up and down the line. Moments later, the resounding orders from the platoon sergeants yelling, "Get up and move out!" rang out. The soldiers got up, picked up their gear, got in line and started the march once again down the hot, miserable, dusty road. Sam recalled later, "There was no time for remorse, reflection or grieving. We were now a machine programed to carry on despite the circumstances." Though the screams, smells and carnage of that day did not seem to fully resonate in his consciousness that day, his unconscious mind certainly recorded them. This experience led to his reoccurring nightmares and challenges with PTSD (Post Traumatic Stress Disorder) that he has had **to** learn to live with over the years. While some of the symptoms and reactions related to the Bougainville road attack have subsided over the years, Sam occasionally still has nightmares or becomes anxious and nervous when certain triggers set him off. During these episodes, he vividly sees the gory scene and the suffering on the faces of the bullet-riddled bodies of his fellow soldiers who were not as fortunate as he was.

Guam

Samuel and a fellow Code Talker found themselves pinned down behind a downed palm tree on Agat Beach on the island of Guam in the summer of 1944. The enemy was well fortified in natural and manmade caves. Snipers in the trees had everyone on edge. Finally, after several tense moments with shots ricocheting off the tree where they were hiding, they had enough. Sam decided he would quickly move towards another downed tree, hoping it would distract the sniper long enough for his partner to take out the sniper. Sam took off, dove over the trunk of the tree, and heard a shot ring out from the sniper, which thankfully missed him. However, a second shot from his comrade's gun found the intended target and the sniper fell to the ground. Once again the marksmanship they had learned on the reservation paid off and the wild horse game from his school days came in handy. The code was a key player in the ultimate success at Guam according to Samuel. Because of the strategic vantage points and the mountainous terrain overlooking the beach invasion, it was vital that the communication between U.S troops, not be compromised. For the U.S. invasion and the ultimate taking of the island, it was crucial to keep the Japanese guessing about the maneuvers of the Marines and U.S.

Navy. The Code was working with precision and speed, which ended up being a significant combat advantage for the U.S, since the Japanese had the artillery high ground, plus countless interlocking caves awaiting them just off the beach area. Due to the joint efforts of the Code Talkers fully employing the Code and fierce fighting from the Marines, the Allies were able to position their artillery and tank support for a successful advance and eventual victory over the Japanese strong holds. It was exhilarating for the Code Talkers to experience this new tactical communication weapon in action and gratifying to see how their hard work was successfully assisting in the war efforts and saving lives.

Peleliu

Peleliu Island was the next challenge for the Marines in September of 1944. Sam recalls this being a difficult island to navigate because of the rugged and unforgiving terrain. The enemy dug into the volcanic catacombs within the cliffs and hills. The Marines spent multiple grueling days marching from cave to cave on a mission to destroy them. Often, the Japanese refused to leave the caves and, as a result, the caves became their graves. On Peleliu, Sam experienced more tragedies of war first-hand. He and another Code Talker were on guard duty, positioned high on a cliff overlooking railroad tracks that ran from one end of the clearing to the other. It was early morning and a fog hovered over the area making visibility difficult. Out of the fog, two figures appeared from the jungle on the opposite side of the clearing from where they were dug in with a BAR. The figures reminded Sam of ghosts because they appeared solid white due to the fog and the lack of visual clarity from their position. They both yelled for the slow-moving figures to halt and identify themselves. The two figures did pause, but continued their approach. After several more warnings, the figures continued moving closer. Finally, they had no choice but to open fire on the two shadowy persons advancing into the restricted area in front of their position. Tragically, they found out later the victims were two Japanese nurses dressed in their white uniforms. No one will ever know if they were planning to surrender and did not understand the orders, or if it was a decoy commonly used by the Japanese army to discover the location of the guards. Regardless, that episode continues to haunt Sam to this day.

The island was not completely stabilized by the end of November, but great progress had been made with minimal resistance. The Marines were making preparations to celebrate Thanksgiving. The Code Talkers decided to add goat stew, a Navajo favorite, to the menu. While it smelled wonderful, the fact that they used virtually the whole animal to make the stew made it rather unappetizing to everyone but the Navajos. As the unit was about to sit down to eat, a Japanese *Zero* spoiled the celebration by making a pass and destroying most of the meal. The soldiers were unscathed, but after the dust settled, it was discovered that only the goat stew survived - and was now the main course! After the meal, those who ate it enthusiastically admitted they liked it. The Navajos could not resist promoting the stew as the source of their great strength and courage!

Okinawa

In many ways, Okinawa, Sam's last campaign, was his most difficult both mentally and physically. The landing was a complete surprise with relatively no resistance compared to other invasions, which lead to a false sense of victory for the troops. During the next few weeks, a couple of important things took place: a significant portion of the island was secured and the troops were well rested - exactly what they needed due to what lay ahead for them. The wakeup call came when the Navy encountered a fierce air attack from a desperate Japanese nation. Wave after wave of kamikaze pilots hit the U.S. Navy force off the coast of Okinawa. Shortly after these naval attacks, the Japanese ground forces opened up on the advancing Marine force. The last holdout on the island was a mountainous area that was heavily fortified with a seemingly endless cave system, interlocking tunnels and tactical vantage points for the Japanese. While the U.S. patrols had an idea they were finally approaching the Japanese force on the island, they could not have foreseen the horrendous experiences they would have to endure. Because of the tactical advantage of the Japanese, the Code was once again instrumental in helping the Allies gain some counter advantages during this fierce battle. Make no mistake: while the Code aided in the success, the real triumph came through the execution of the communications and orders relayed to the fighting soldiers on the ground, air and sea. One can only imagine the brutality and carnage Sam and his fellow Marines had to endure during the taking of Okinawa. Samuel thought Guam and Peleliu were horrific, but those battles were a walk in the park compared to Okinawa. Over the years, he often has commented that he has experienced what hell is like - and you do not want to go there. Sam lost many of his fellow Marines during this campaign. Looking back is difficult as he sees that the Japanese surrender took place just a short time after many of these soldiers lost their lives. He is not aware of any Code Talkers that lost their lives on Okinawa, but he can recall many young soldiers who would never get a chance to return home to their loved ones. Those who did make it back would be forever changed due to the things they saw and events they lived through. One can never erase the visions so traumatically burned into their minds. Sam is very thankful that the war ended after Okinawa and that they were spared from an invasion of the island of Japan. He recalls discussions among the brass and his fellow troops noting that Japan was the next leg in this costly journey to victory and that Okinawa would be considered a picnic compared to the invasion on the mainland. Sam could not conceive how such a battle could be as bad as what he just experienced… but that is also what he thought after walking onto the beaches at Peleliu. Malula notices that when Sam shares about Okinawa with her privately, he is transformed back to his 20-year-old mind. Vivid memories come flooding back as though those horrifying events happened just recently. She feels blessed that he is comfortable sharing these memories with her and is convinced that these mini-therapeutic sessions are beneficial to him as he continues to journey through the healing process.

Rest Camp

Rest Camp, as described by Sam, consisted of sleep, recreation, training, and more training. They had all the provisions they needed at most of his R & R locations: food, cigarettes, beer and ample amounts of coconuts and bananas. Recreation consisted of every form of game involving balls including: baseball, kickball, soccer, and occasionally basketball and football. Soldiers made up creative games that included multiple items and rules - anything to keep their minds active but relaxed. Since one of the requirements of the Marines was the ability to swim, Sam took advantage of every opportunity to improve his skills. He recalls a river that ran through the island on Guadalcanal that was very popular. He and his sergeant spent time unwinding by jumping off the deep ravines into the cool water. Swimming was limited to fresh water venues since unsafe currents and the threat of sharks made oceans less than ideal. Swimming was a treat for Sam and his comrades since it was not a common activity in the desert Southwest. Other pastimes included an occasional fishing trip, boat construction, and the making of handcrafted items with the locals.

Training continued for the Code Talkers and consisted of practicing the code over and over, adding new words to keep pace with new equipment and new fighting techniques, and staying abreast of the ever-changing enemy tactics. At times it seemed a daunting task. It was critical to remain physically fit and there were also scheduled times for tactical practice maneuvers to prepare for the constantly changing enemy tactics.

During this time of rest, the Navajos spent time devouring news from home by sharing stories and information received through letters from family and friends. The letters were usually three months old due to the normal challenges of the military censoring process and of locating the recipients. Sam wrote back when he could, and sent $45 of his monthly salary of $50 to help the family. He kept $5 for spending money, plenty for him since most everything was provided by the military. He made a little extra on the side by selling his rations of beer and cigarettes since he had no use for them. On a rare occasion, the Navajos would cook up a batch of goat stew to remind them of home.

Sam was afforded a treat while resting on Guadalcanal when Navajos from other units on the island came to visit the Code Talkers. He was overjoyed at the chance to spend time with three of his cousins from home. Two were brothers serving in the Army Infantry and the other was serving in the Navy and was stationed on Guadalcanal. This was a welcome and needed morale boost for the foreign boys from the Four Corners area. Even today, as Sam describes this opportunity to see family, it is obvious the positive impact it made on him. Toward the end of the war, the news that one of the brothers had been killed in action made this time they had had together that much more meaningful.

The End of the War

The Army dealt with remaining resistance, and the Marines regrouped and headed for the their next destination. While on the way, Samuel and the other soldiers were informed of the surrender of the Japanese Empire. They returned to Okinawa where Sam was assigned to recovery duty and instructed to wait for his next orders. Would he be sent home or would he be assigned to a new island? Eventually, he was told that he would be going to China in "two weeks." From Sam's vantage point, it seemed the Marines had their own time frame… "Two weeks" might mean anything from one month to six months! After a month Sam was on a "slow boat to China." With the massive drawdown that was occurring in the military, Sam was not sure what his duties would look like. He spent several months in China with no specific orders or mission. Finally, his commanding officer asked him if would be interested in signing up for four more years and if he would consider a career with the military. Sam respectfully declined stating that he missed his home and that he had had enough of war. In January of 1946, he was discharged after nearly three years of service. He felt like he had aged much more than four years and he was in need of physical, emotional and spiritual rest.

Hazards of War

War can easily become something like multiple matches of chess. After each massive battle, both sides learn the tactics of the other side and use what they learn to change their maneuvers in an attempt to gain the advantage for the next battle. In the European Campaign, for example, the Allies had to change their tactics in how they approached hedgerow fighting because their first attempts had ended with high casualty rates. They changed their strategies through troop movements and mechanical ingenuity, which lowered the casualty rate. Similar "chess games" took place in the Pacific Conflict between the Allies and the Japanese. Sam noticed a change in tactics from his first campaign on Guadalcanal to the campaign on Guam. The mounting losses experienced by the Empire of Japan left them more motivated and more desperate. The Japanese soldier became focused on sacrificing his own life in a suicidal manner, with complete disregard for self. Sam remembers the night attacks on Guam became more frequent and more brutal and that they had a physiological toll on U.S troops. The Japanese were very quiet on one raid and on the next they would yell at the top of their lungs and charge smashing into the lines. Hand-to-hand combat occurred night after night. Sometimes the Japanese soldiers would dress like U.S. soldiers and infiltrate the ranks, catching the troops off guard. American troops began to second-guess the shadowy figures coming near them, a problem which could have led to deadly consequences for friends instead of the targeted foe. The dark quiet nights were the worst because even the slightest sound had the soldiers on edge; they would try to relax only to hear another sound putting them into an exhausting adrenaline cycle. Continued exposure to this cycle left even the most hardened warrior in an unhealthy and sometimes dangerous psychotic state. Sam attributes the challenges with his psychological recovery after returning from the war to these unnatural, stressful experiences. He had difficulty relaxing and sleeping and constantly woke up to both normal and imaginary sounds at night, setting off the cycle once again. Night shadows were also problematic, as he found himself panicking and responding with a cold sweat. Despite his challenges with the symptoms of PTSD, he still feels blessed because some of his companions either went crazy or took their own lives to cope with the pain.

Lessons Learned

Sam perceives many parallels between the Navajo traditions and the accomplishments of the Code Talkers between 1942 and 1945. The Navajo creation story tells of a monster slaughtering their ancestors and twin warriors called to fight the monster and save the people. After a fierce battle the twins were able to defeat the monster through their brave efforts and their skill with weapons. The Navajo Code Talkers (warriors in the creation story) were a group of brave men who creatively used skills with their language to help in the defeat of the monster (the Japanese Empire) who was threatening their land and killing their people. Not only were they fighting for the United states, they were fighting on behalf Navajos (over 15,000) who served in WWII and for the honor of the Navajo people. On the Navajo Reservation, towering over the desert, are twin rock formations, which are reminiscent of the twin warriors of the creation story.

The obvious casualties of war are those who have served the military in battle and paid the highest price with their lives. But others have also paid a dear price. Collateral damage from war includes soldiers with both physical and emotional scars, impacting the quality and length of the soldiers' lives. Obvious cases are those who lost limbs or experienced impairments as a result of battle trauma. Less obvious are those soldiers who come home to fight PTSD (more commonly labeled "battle fatigue" following WWII) and those who contracted diseases that left them debilitated or shortened their lives. Sam remembers the impact that diseases such as malaria and typhoid had on the troops. He also knew of instances where soldiers could not take the pressure of battle and committed suicide, either through the use of a weapon or by ingesting medical alcohol taken from the medical supplies.

Reflections

Sam often emphasizes the enormous, complex task of developing the code, since there was no written Navajo alphabet or language. The challenge was similar to putting a puzzle together without all of the pieces and without seeing what the finished picture would look like. An example of the linguistic challenge these young men tackled took place in the editing studio when making *The Heart of a Warrior* documentary. A Navajo student, familiar with the "old" or traditional Navajo language and also with the more contemporary Navajo language, was assisting the crew. Like Sam, this student grew up spending hours listening to his grandparents tell the old stories. We asked him to translate a short paragraph of Sam's words from Navajo to English for the documentary. Throughout the process, the student kept apologizing for taking so long to make the translation. After about three hours of work, he told us it was close enough and handed us a short paragraph translated into English. He explained the complexity of translating from Navajo to English with a grammar analogy: "Imagine a paragraph in English describing a family event. Now, take all of the nouns from the paragraph and place them one after another. Then take all the verbs and place them one after another. Do the same with the adverbs and continue with each part of speech." He continued, "That is how you would write that same paragraph in the Navajo language. If you were to read that paragraph to a person who understood and spoke fluent Navajo, they would understand what you said." He felt sure most Navajo would understand the not-so-perfect English translation, which would be used in the documentary. The original creators of the code would probably not have imagined that the enemy would be unable to crack the code and that to this day, over 70 years later, it still has not been broken.

While Samuel did not experience any overt racial discrimination, it did exist. As far as he knows from his research, only one Code Talker was promoted to a position beyond corporal, although many had enough points to qualify. Caucasian soldiers with fewer points and much less experience were consistently promoted, while the Navajo Code Talkers were passed over. Other discrimination came through stereotypes and derogatory comments. This is typical military ribbing, but nonetheless the negative comments were directed towards Native Americans. Sam recalls a sergeant in Bougainville who regularly irritated one of his comrades by referring to him as "chief." While this may sound trivial, the sergeant was not using the name in a respectful manner. His tone of voice and his mannerisms in front of the other men made it very clear his words were not complimentary. At some point, the Code Talker had enough and, after being called "chief" once again, commented, "If I was the chief, we would not be in this mess." He was not called "chief" again. Another example of the stereotypical messages was printed on the cover of the Navajo Code Manual with its cartoon-style Native Americans commenting to one another. While these insensitive forms of communication were more obvious, the Code Talkers also felt a more subtle isolation from the general military population. Sam admits he is not sure whether the isolation was deliberate because they were Native Americans, or if it was due to the secrecy of the code.

Platoon photo. Sam is on the front row, first soldier on the far right. (Photo from Samuel's Code Talker Scrapbook)

Sam's Marine photo. (Family photo)

Photo of Sam's drill sergeant. (Photo from the sergeant's daughter given to Sam)

Sam (right) headed to Guadalcanal. (Photo from Samuel's Code Talker Scrapbook)

Sam at the remains of a Japanese temple on Guam, 1944. (Photo from Samuel's Code Talker Scrapbook)

Newspaper clippings of Code Talker photos from the National Archives. (From Sam's Code Talker Scrapbook)

NAVAJO DICTIONARY ALPHABET

Letter	Word	(Navajo)
A.	ANT	(WOL-LA-CHEE)
A.	APPLE	(BE-LA-SANA)
A.	AXE	(TSE-NILL)
B.	BADGER	(NA-HASH-CHID)
B.	BEAR	(SHUSH)
B.	BARREL	(TOISH-JEH)
C.	CAT	(MOASI)
C.	COAL	(TLA-GIN)
C.	COW	(BA-GOSHI)
D.	DEER	(BE)
D.	DEVIL	(CHINDI)
D.	DOG	(LHA-CHA-EH)
E.	EAR	(AH-JAH)
E.	ELK	(DZEH)
E.	EYE	(AH-NAH)
F.	FIR	(CHUO)
F.	FLY	(TSA-E-DONIN-EE)
F.	FOX	(MA-E)
G.	GIRL	(AH-TAD)
G.	GOAT	(KLIZZIE)
G.	GUM	(JEHA)
H.	HAIR	(TSE-GAH)
H.	HAT	(CHA)
H.	HORSE	(LIN)
I.	ICE	(TKIN)
I.	ITCH	(YEH-HES)
I.	INTESTINE	(A-CHI)
J.	JACKASS	(TKELE-CHO-GI)
J.	JAW	(AH-YA-TSINNE)
J.	JERK	(YIL-DO-I)
K.	KETTLE	(AD-HO-LON)
K.	KEY	(BA-AH-NE-DI-TININ)
K.	KID	(KLIZZIE-YAZZIE)
L.	LAMB	(DIBEH-YAZZIE)
L.	LEG	(AH-JAD)
L.	LION	(NASH-DOIE-TSO)
M.	MATCH	(TSIN-TLITI)
M.	MIRROR	(BE-TAS-TNI)
M.	MOUSE	(NA-AS-TSO-SI)
N.	NEEDLE	(TSAH)
N.	NOSE	(A-CHIN)
O.	OIL	(A-KHA)
O.	ONION	(TLO-CHIN)
O.	OWL	(NE-AHS-JAH)
P.	PANT	(CLA-GI-AIH)
P.	PIG	(BI-SO-DIH)
P.	PRETTY	(NE-ZHONI)
Q.	QUIVER	(CA-YEILTH)
R.	RABBIT	(GAH)
R.	RAM	(DAH-NES-TSA)
R.	RICE	(AH-LOSZ)
S.	SHEEP	(DIBEH)
S.	SNAKE	(KLESH)
T.	TEA	(D-AH)
T.	TOOTH	(A-WOH)
T.	TURKEY	(THAN-ZIE)
U.	UNCLE	(SHI-DA)
U.	UTE	(NO-DA-JH)
V.	VICTOR	(A-KEH-DI-GLINI)
W.	WEASEL	(GLOE-IH)
X.	CROSS	(AL-NA-AS-DZOH)
Y.	YUCCA	(TSAH-AS-ZIH)
Z.	ZINC	(BESH-DO-TLIZ)
O.	OBOE	
P.	PETER	
Q.	QUEEN	
R.	ROGER	
S.	SUGAR	
T.	TARE	
A.	ABLE	
B.	BAKER	
C.	CHARLIE	
D.	DOG	
E.	EASY	
F.	FOX	
G.	GEORGE	
H.	HOW	
I.	ITEM	
J.	JIG	
K.	KING	
L.	LOVE	
M.	MIKE	
N.	NAN	
U.	UNCLE	
V.	VICTOR	
W.	WILLIAM	
X.	X-RAY	
Y.	YOKE	
Z.	ZEBRA	

Cover and first page of the Navajo Dictionary. (Copy from Samuel's Code Talker Scrapbook)

Chapter Four

Healing and Purpose

One of Samuels's favorite Hymns: *Where Could I Go*

"We were in what is now called the Buffalo Mountain area, just southwest of Shiprock, where I was working on the surveyor's crew for a road construction company when we had daily encounters with some pesky bears. We left our camp to go out on the job and came back in the early evening to find bears had ransacked our camp. We tried multiple strategies to discourage them with limited success. Eventually, we moved down the road and apparently out of their territory. We were relieved, because it got old working hard all day and then having to spend hours cleaning up the mess they left for us." (Sam's memory from his job on a survey crew following the war.)

Over the centuries, hundreds of thousands of soldiers before and after Samuel Sandoval have had two things in common. First, when they made it back from war, they counted their blessings that they survived and second, they had the daunting task of trying to put their lives back together. In Sam's case, he left for the war as an innocent and naïve young man and came back aged emotionally – a 40-year-old man in a 23-year-old body. The abnormal maturation that occurred as a result of his experiences at war would have dramatic, lingering effects on his transition from military to civilian life.

Samuel's glorified expectations of war were quickly shattered when he first stepped on a South Pacific island and had to dodge bullets, bombs and bodies. In similar fashion, the great expectations he had of returning home were shattered soon after he arrived back in the Four Corners area of New Mexico. Many things had changed in the three years he had been gone. He expected to return to his old familiar stomping grounds, to a simpler and more tranquil way of life. It didn't take long to see that the government had once again stuck their federal noses into the Navajo way of life. A new law enacted during the war restricted grazing land and land usage on the reservation and surrounding areas. This greatly reduced the number of Navajos who could make a living through agriculture and range management and it left Sam contemplating his next move. His military training did not translate into recognizable skills that fit the civilian world of work, at least not on the reservation. This occupational void, along with the recalibrating of his body, soul and mind from the effects of war in a less-than-supportive civilian environment, left him in a vulnerable state. He soon began to experience unexplainable physical ailments, which eventually left him unable to walk. To accomplish daily tasks, he had to be carried by family members or friends. Countless hours, over a period of several months, were spent visiting medical specialists who were not able to diagnose his condition. Finally, his father convinced him to try the traditional Navajo way of healing. Though hesitant, with memories of his great-grandfather healing in the traditional ways implanted in his mind, Samuel was persuaded.

The Navajo healing process included many traditional ceremonies and also specific procedures individualized for Samuel. Circumstances contributing to the illness were taken into consideration before determining the remedies and prayers to be applied. In Sam's case, those who applied the healing techniques knew that the effects of the war had definitely had a negative impact on his overall health. The intervention would require ten days in the Hogan and treatments of herbs – some applied to his outer extremities and others ingested orally. Hours of prayers were prayed over Sam during this time period. On the tenth day, male members of the healing group rode horses around the Hogan while shooting rifles in the air to scare away the influence of the evil spirits. The designated medicine man came inside the Hogan where Sam was lying on the dirty floor and told him to get up. Sam has no answers for what happened that day nor an understanding of all the mysteries of this traditional way of healing. What he does know is that the medicine man stood over him that night and said, "Get up. You can do it." Sam immediately stood up and walked out of the Hogan unassisted. He never experienced those physical impairments again.

Thankful for the healing he experienced, he still faced a tough journey in his quest for healing from emotional and relational scars. From this time through his early forties, Sam struggled on and off with alcohol which, in turn, had a negative impact on two unsuccessful marriages. His first marriage took place when he was in his early twenties and only lasted a couple of years. Sam was married again in his late twenties and this time children were involved. This relationship did not survive either, and Sam has been estranged from his second wife and his children. He does not readily speak of these relationships, but does admit that the scars of war impacted the intimacy and health of these unsuccessful marriages.

Sam admits there were times he thought about giving up and allowing the ghosts that haunted his mind and spirit to have their way. At times he questioned whether the difficulties in his life were a result of his inability to avoid the sacred "do's and don'ts" he had been taught as a child. He remembered his great-grandfather's admonition about refraining from walking over dead bodies and avoiding human blood in battle and worried that this had somehow doomed him to a life of continual suffering. Were these challenges a result of the time as a child when he and his brother came home with a saddle they had found in the desert? Their grandmother became alarmed and immediately ordered them to return it to where they found it. After returning the saddle, they came home to a calmer Grandmother who explained that they had stumbled upon their grandfather's burial site and, unbeknownst to them, they had disturbed the site. (The traditional means of burial at the time of his grandfather's death was to bury the Navajo man with his saddled horse.)

Despite these questions and setbacks, Sam determined to embrace the struggle, learn from his mistakes, and use the things he learned to help others in similar circumstances. While he would not have chosen to endure the pain of broken relationships, he did not let the past define him, but determined to move forward with an attitude of optimism. He journeyed on; every challenge he faced motivating him to better himself. He knew with God-given strength and wisdom, he could assist others facing broken relationships and substance abuse. Through prayer and worship of God, he began to experience spiritual healing, resulting in peace for his soul.

Sam enrolled at the University of Utah in Salt Lake City to pursue a degree in counseling with a specialization in drug and alcohol counseling. He wanted to give back to the tribe and community. He felt God led him to pursue a degree in the helping professions, as Navajo counselors were desperately needed on the reservation. The combination of a poor economy, a lack of jobs, and federal interference created an environment of social distress in the region. Many resorted to alcohol to numb the effects of poverty, which compounded the stressors on family relationships. Substance abuse was taking a toll on marriages and families. Sam, understanding substance abuse and brokenness firsthand, knew there was an urgent need for individuals who were willing to roll up their sleeves and help. His great-grandfather had devoted his life to the healing of his people during and after the challenges surrounding the Long Walk and now, Sam found himself ready to face a different sort of tragedy attacking the people he loved. This enemy was less obvious, but every bit as sinister and nondiscriminatory in whom it harmed. Sam was not intimidated by the messiness of lives gripped by the devastating effects of alcoholism. He had faced his own battles with alcohol and had survived the horrors of combat. His education had prepared him and his experiences equipped him to pour his life into this work. This was not just a profession for Sam, this was personal and he was willing to fight the enemy with the same energy and passion he had felt when charging onto the South Pacific beaches. He had lived through World War II and survived his own war with alcoholism and he was ready to help others fight and the battles where they found themselves. He was excited to serve the local community that he dearly loved.

After receiving his training in alcohol and substance counseling and working for other agencies, Samuel felt led to start his own clinic/halfway house in the Four Corners area. He found deserted buildings on the edge of Farmington, but had very little capital to purchase the property and no funds to furnish the facilities. His "can do" attitude from his Marine training kicked into gear. Sam approached the mayor of the city asking him to donate unused city furniture and to run the gas lines needed for the facility. The mayor was willing to help, *until* he found out that Sam would be serving *everyone* who walked in the doors, not just the Native American population. So the first round of this skirmish ended with Sam temporally in retreat, but by no means admitting defeat. It would have been easier for Sam to give in to the mayor's demands, but Sam was well aware of the hurting culture he felt called to serve and knew he must heed the call for diversity and inclusion.

His broad vision for assisting hurting people came from his experiences during the war as he learned about different races, ethnicities and cultures. He had empathized with the natives on each island he was stationed on as he learned of their plight and their desire to take back their land. He felt an obligation to do his part to restore each unique island and culture to its native people. He was often reminded of the battles his own Navajo people had fought and the trials they endured as they endeavored to retain their lands and way of life. The stories his great-grandfather told of how the Navajo people had remained strong and proud, and how they had persevered through trials, once again filled Sam's mind. There he was in the South Pacific helping to free strange tribes who, after further thought, were similar to his own tribe. The biggest difference was that vast turquoise waters surrounded these tribes, while breath-taking deserts surrounded his tribe.

Sam grew up in a culture where one had to adapt to overcome adversity and survive. This made him well-suited for the tactical maneuvering necessary to endure and survive war. His military experience was invaluable as he learned to strategically manage the civilian and political obstacles that were in opposition to his dreams. He had come too far and lived through too many hard times to allow this "monster" to stop him from doing the right thing to help his community. Resembling a brave and courageous Code Talker, he overcame the political "monsters" with language through action. He decided to organize a benefit dinner and he invited many influential people in the community, including the mayor. The politically savvy mayor would have preferred not to attend, but was compelled to because his lack of attendance would be seen as a black mark on his civil servant record. The mayor was wise enough to know that he needed to show his support by being there even though his intentions were to leave his fiscal support at home. The evening dinner and program at Sam's halfway house, as he described it, were a success. Not only did he receive overwhelming support from those in attendance, the mayor told Sam afterwards that he would have a crew there the next day to hook up the gas line and would donate any furniture Sam needed from the warehouse. Within a few weeks, the halfway house was open for business, serving individuals, couples and families. Sam's academic degrees and spiritual growth, along with his own personal experiences, positioned him to become a healer in his community. He was following in the footsteps of his great-grandfather through his roles as warrior, Code Talker, and counselor – a 20th Century medicine man.

When Samuel opened his therapy practice, he adopted the Navajo Code Talker motto as his mission statement: *We defeated the enemy with our language.* He treated a variety of enemies (dysfunctions, trauma and addictions) that were harmful and destructive in the lives of individuals, couples and families. He was convinced that effective communication/language in any relationship system was the key to defeating the enemies targeting the lives of his clients. He made it his therapeutic focus to break the dysfunctional codes in the relationships and establish healthier forms of communication and intimacy. Similar to the operation of the code during the war, Samuel learned the importance of being receptive and flexible in his mission to break the dysfunctional codes/behaviors of his clients. Most of his clients were Native Americans, but due to his experience with different populations during the war, he was welcoming and well equipped to assist people of many diverse backgrounds. It is his belief that the combination of God's grace, the hard work of his clients and his unyielding tenacity as a counselor led to many success stories.

During these satisfying and impactful years in the community, Sam unexpectedly received a tremendous personal blessing when he hired a young Navajo woman to work in his office. As they worked together over the weeks and months, they realized that their feelings for each other went much deeper than friendship. Obstacles in their relationship seemed almost insurmountable, particularly because of the difference in their ages. After much discussion and prayer, they informed others of their intention to become engaged. Malula remembers that, "things did not go as smooth when we let others know of our desire to marry." A handful of friends and family opposed their marriage and others said it wouldn't last due to the age difference, but many others agreed that they made a great couple. Three years after they met, they married on February 16, 1990, at Bethel Christian Reformed Church in Shiprock, New Mexico, in the presence of many supportive friends and family. Malula became his life partner and is the love of his life. The marriage *has* lasted – nearly 30 years - and they are still in love. Because of Sam's age, Malula worries about him, but he keeps assuring her that he plans to outlive his great-grandfather. His optimism does not always chase away her concern for him or the empty feeling that grips her heart thinking about the day when he might not be at her side. One only has to visit with Malula for a short time to see the passion in her tear-filled eyes and to hear her soft, broken speech when expressing her love for Sam; as she puts it, "I love this man."

Malula greatly appreciates and admires the Code Talkers. When she was a young girl, she marveled as she watched the Code Talkers march in local parades. She repeatedly asked her father to tell her the story of the Code Talkers and what their legacy meant to the Navajo tribe. When she met Sam, she had no idea he was a Code Talker; he was her boss and the leader of the halfway house. As they spent more time together, he began to reveal more information about his past. Malula is still in awe that she is married to a Navajo Code Talker! For over 30 years, she has passionately performed the role of the unofficial archivist of the Code Talkers. She has spent countless hours collecting newspaper articles, filming Code Talker events and attending their informal gatherings. She was always at Sam's side when he spoke at events across the country and around the globe, usually helping with logistics and managing the recording of the event. She is the Code Talker taxi driver for many events held in local churches, schools, libraries and communities. She promotes the Navajo Code Talkers, as well as the Navajo culture and language. Alongside her husband, she shares a deep desire to make sure the "Navajo way" does not fade into obscurity.

Lessons Learned

At an early age Sam learned much about life and the Navajo way from the stories told by his relatives, from working on the family ranch and from classmates at his school. He learned that discipline, perseverance, tradition, integrity, honor and loyalty – "the do's and don'ts" - are to be emulated and cherished. The battles he fought in the Pacific and the domestic and personal skirmishes he fought following the war are where he learned to apply the important things he learned as a boy. It's one thing to learn those admirable qualities, but a completely different thing to be able to apply them during the happy times and when facing the trials of life. While he has not mastered the application of these virtues in every situation, he has learned to live life under God's mercy and grace. He has not allowed life's adversities to stop him from doing the right thing. In his quest to open the halfway house, the easiest thing would have been to accept the dismissal from the mayor and move on. However, his inner voice and intestinal fortitude would not let him rest until he did the right thing. It would have been easy for his great-grandfather to give up at Bosco Redondo and forgo the brutal return to the their land and the rebuilding of the Navajo Nation. It seems it is in Sam's DNA to endure the horrors of war, to persevere through his "battle fatigue," to grow from his domestic struggles and to give back to the Navajo Nation. Sam, again referring back to the creation story, believes that the Navajo Nation will continue to defeat its monsters and endure, just as the twins did before his time and before his great-grandfather's time.

Reflection

"This is my story." (Samuel Sandoval)

I have no doubt there are hundreds of compelling stories about each one of the Code Talkers. Sam has shared his story, but reminds me that he is telling his story and not speaking for others. Others must share their stories. To speak for others dishonors their stories and voices. I can only hope and pray I have accurately represented Sam's story and that the words printed here are an accurate reflection of his heart. Having said that, I must confess that one needs the opportunity to visit with Sam in person to fully grasp the passion he has for his Savior, Jesus Christ, his wife, Malula, his family, the Code Talkers and the Navajo Nation. It is the whole of those parts of Sam that drives him to continue in his journey to influence and encourage the Navajo Nation to continue to embrace their language, traditions and culture. The "Navajo way" must endure for the health and good of the nation. I am thankful for the privilege of spending time with Sam in his home, at the studio, on location, on the phone and over meals; this is where I was able to get a true glimpse of the heart of this warrior. I have seen the tears in his eyes as he retells his great-grandfather's stories and his war experiences. I have sensed the honor he felt as he received the Silver Medal. I have heard the passion in his voice as he reflects on his devotion for Malula, his love for his brother, Merril, and his respect for his fellow Code Talkers. I am a better person as a result of knowing the warrior, Samuel Sandoval. He has taught me to embrace the challenges I face with an optimistic attitude and with the goal of growing as a person. He has reminded me that the things I learn through adversity can be used to positively impact others I encounter facing similar challenges.

Looking towards Shiprock from Buffalo Pass. (JCCC photo)

Sam served in the Hall of the Chapter Building near the Checkerboard area. (JCCC Photo)

Campsite where the bears ransacked their tents. (JCCC photo)

Photo of Sam shortly after receiving his Masters in Counseling. (Family photo)

Engagement photo of Sam and Malula. (Family photo)

Wedding photo of Sam and Malula. (Family photo)

Sam and Malula at a luncheon following a Code Talker event. (Family photo)

Signing autographs after speaking on the Guam trip. (Family photo)

Autographs after speaking at a local grade school. (Family photo)

Chapter Five

Legacy

> *I was not completely sure how I would respond while watching the premier of the motion picture, "Wind Talkers," the story of the Navajo Code Talkers. While some parts were accurate, my wife and I had to chuckle at some of Hollywood's version of our story. At one part of the movie, just before an intense battle, one of the Code Talkers decided to symbolically wear a pair of moccasins into battle. I could not help myself while watching the scene, I leaned over to Malula and told her, "I don't recall wearing moccasins in the war." She laughed. I doubt any Code Talker would have worn such unsafe footwear in such a brutal and unforgiving environment as what we experienced in battle. Moccasins would not have been the ideal footwear to use.* (Memory from Samuel)

Sam and Malula would probably not use the word "leisurely" to describe their retirement years, and they would have it no other way. There is too much to be accomplished to sit back and relax. Their quest to serve the community and the Code Talkers keep them on the move.

Most of Sam's time has been devoted to the Navajo Code Talker Association and story. A historic reunion of Code Talkers was held in 1974 in Window Rock, Arizona, capital of the Navajo Nation. The Navajo Code Talker

Association, a non-profit organization, was established at this gathering and the details of the official Code Talker uniform were chosen. Sam has attended countless Code Talker events, participated in community parades, served as speaker for many events, taken part in autograph sessions and is always willing to be interviewed by the occasional reporter who stops by to hear his story. He has been active on the speaking circuit and relishes the opportunity to speak about the Navajo culture and language and his experience as a Code Talker. He wears his official Navajo uniform with the Code Talker patch and one of his Marine Corps caps, and speaks to the significance of the uniform's colors and symbolism as they relate to Navajo Nation. Listed below are the components of the code talker uniform and their meaning:

- Bright yellow shirt – Symbolizes corn pollen. Its significance is related to the natural fertilization process and the honoring and celebration of life.
- Khaki pants – The khaki color reflects the soil and Mother Earth.
- Black Shoes – Black is one of the Navajo's sacred colors.
- Red Hat with Marine Corps patch – Recognition of the Marines Corps and their rich traditions.
- Code Talker patch worn on the right sleeve – Symbolizes the fight between the warrior twins and the monster. It includes the four sacred colors of black, blue, yellow and white. These colors are also linked to the variety of colors found in corn.

Sam recalls the many delays by the government in recognizing the contribution of the Code Talkers in WWII.

It was many years after the war before the public really understood their valiant role. One reason for delay was the secrecy of the code. The Code Talkers were strictly warned not to speak about the code or "talk code" after being discharged from the military. After the war, many of the young Navajos went back to their normal routine of life on the reservation where they had many occasions to run into fellow Code Talkers. It is humorous to hear Sam tell how they would not speak a word about the code even among themselves. They had an unspoken pact that they would not speak in code or even converse about the code. Sam believes that their mistrust of the U.S government contributed to their paranoia of being arrested if they were to break the silence of the code. The code was declassified in 1968, and they finally began to be more comfortable discussing the war and the code amongst themselves, although Sam indicated that they were still hesitant to discuss it because they took their orders from the military very seriously.

Recognition for the contributions made by the Code Talkers was slow in coming. This became a concern of Samuel's as more and more members of the elite group began experiencing health issues and passing away. Finally, in July of 2001, 56 years after the end of World War II, the original 29 Code Talkers were awarded the Congressional Gold Medal, and in November of the same year the rest of the original 80 Code Talkers were awarded the Congressional Silver Medal. A sign on the stage, which was filled with dignitaries, read "Diné Bizaad Yee Atah Naayéé' Yik'eh Deesdlíí," which translated reads, "The Navajo language was used to defeat the enemy." This inscription was also engraved on the medals received by the Code Talkers.

In 2005, a group of Navajo Code Talkers had the opportunity to visit the beautiful island of Guam in celebration of the liberation of the island. Guam government officials and a film crew toured significant battle locations on the beaches and at Japanese strategic strongholds in the hills and cliffs. Green Beach, the military name for the beach where they landed, looked much different than the images ingrained in his mind from when he was 19. It took time to re-orient his brain in order to recognize anything familiar. Sam viewed the beach through the eyes of an old warrior and saw a peaceful scene with clear waters, sprawling palm trees and lush undergrowth, but he quickly became overwhelmed by the memories of the landing and the gruesome carnage he had seen in this place. Standing in front of the signage in the small park area brought back a flood of memories from the day that he and thousands of other Marines charged onto the beach desperately searching for cover. The only remnants remaining of the horror of that day were an old Japanese concrete pill box, now five feet offshore, a Japanese anti-aircraft gun and many man-made cave entrances in the distance, which had helped to slow down and repel the Marines advances. As Malula filmed and Sam slowly walked the beach, you could tell by his expression, he was drawn back into a world only he could enter. He made narrative comments, pointing out a few areas where he and his comrades struggled to survive. You could tell by the fluctuations in his voice and the stream of tears flowing down his checks that the memories were very real even though it had taken place over 60 years earlier. He dried the tears he shed for his comrades who lost their lives during the assault and in the following weeks with a clean, white handkerchief. As a part of the healing process, he took a jar and scooped up some sand and seashells from the beach. He placed the handkerchief he had just used to remove his tears in the jar. Today that jar sits on a shelf in his home with hundreds of other items commemorating his military service and the service of his fellow Code Talkers. Later, he reflected how he was caught off guard by the barrage of memories.

Recently while in the studio watching the video Malula had filmed on their celebration trip to Guam, Samuel had difficulty talking as the memories flooded his mind. You could sense the pain and agony in his voice as he described different events - the jump into the cold seawater, the struggle to escape away from the open space on the beach in order to reach more secure place, the fear he felt while dodging sniper fire, fighting against the stubborn Japanese in their caves and tunnels, repelling counter attacks, the unnerving nights of guard duty, and finally waiting for the army to arrive for cleanup duty.

Both before and following his retirement, Sam was active in the local Shiprock Chapter, a part of the Navajo Nation community government, serving as vice president from 1989-1994. "They love me here," he said as he talked about his participation in chapter events. His family has a rich history of participating in the local chapters in the Shiprock and Checkerboard areas near his old homestead and close to Turtle Mountain. He remembers that the beginnings of what are now well-established chapters were once trading posts. He recalls stopping by the trading posts as a child with his family and getting to choose a treat of some kind, usually candy or gum. While Sam did not particularly like the politics of the chapter work, he reminded those who seemed to enjoy the political games that the chapter must focus its energy and resources to serve the community and its members. Even today he stays informed on the politics of the Navajo Nation, though he grows weary of those who think too highly of themselves and who seem to forget the people they were elected to serve. He was especially disappointed when a seemingly perfect opportunity presented itself for a Navajo Code Talker museum to be built just outside the Navajo capital of Window Rock. Land had been designated for this project and the architectural drawings had been submitted. Unfortunately the funds were not used in an efficient manner and the project was put on hold, with no projected future date to proceed with the plans. While these types of political blunders frustrate him, they do not keep him from promoting efforts to improve the local community when given the opportunity to share his opinion. He has hopes that there will someday be a Code Talker museum where memorabilia can be displayed. He hopes to be in attendance at the grand opening.

Whenever Sam and Malula get a chance, they make the beautiful trip from Shiprock to Window Rock to reflect and pray for family, friends and their community. While he does not need to come to this sacred place to pray and reflect, there is a different atmosphere in and around Window Rock. Not only is it the center of the Navajo government and the heart of the Navajo history, traditions and values are represented here. Code Talkers and their families have shared countless events and gatherings in the Window Rock area. In sight of the Window Rock Monument are the Window Rock Visitor Center and the Navajo Nation government offices.

At the base of Window Rock is the Code Talker Memorial. Sam never tires of viewing both structures - one built by the hands of God and the other sculptured by the hands of men. During the filming of *The Heart of a Warrior* at Window Rock, Sam proudly shared the monument with the film crew and spoke about the area and its significance to the Navajo people and to him, personally. The Code Talker Memorial is a statue of a Code Talker in battle uniform positioned on one knee speaking on a radio with a paratrooper M1 Carbine rifle by his side. At the base of the memorial are bricks with the names of the Code Talkers inscribed on them. Sam eagerly hunts for the names of the friends, including the names of the young men who were pictured with him on the front porch of the Navajo Methodist Mission School in 1943. He also seeks the brick inscribed with his name, Samuel F. Sandoval, and the brick inscribed with the name of his brother, Merril Sandoval. Sadly, not many of those he searched for were still living at that time, but he enjoyed telling stories of their school days and happenings on the reservation, about their bravery during the war and of their participation in Code Talker events.

When visiting the Code Talker Memorial, Malula usually sits on a bench by herself to allow Sam time to reflect and process the memories in private. During this time she usually takes a moment to reflect how God spared his life through the war and how blessed she is to have Sam in her life. After hearing all the horrific stories over the years, she says, "Okinawa was a bloodbath, the largest amphibious landing invasion in the South Pacific. God spared my husband Samuel's life; he almost never came back from Okinawa. As a wife it is hard to bear the sensitive, emotional, pain; it rips my heart and just has to come out in tears. There is more, so painful to share, I think only this I'll put across. This I will cherish to the last day of my breath." She will eventually join him and he often shares some of reflections. As they return to the bench and sit together holding hands, she will listen intently and comfort him in ways only she can.

In recent years, Sam has not attended as many Code Talker events as he used to. He rarely travels any distance that will keep him away from home for more than a day. Because he is not able to get out as much, he loves for others to visit him at his home on the edge of town in Shiprock. He can often be found sitting on his back patio looking towards the beautiful Buffalo Mountain area and the towering formation of Shiprock itself. A visitor to the neighborhood would note that the Sandoval house has the American and Marine flags flying proudly in the front yard. Multiple rooms in the home are decorated with Code Talker memorabilia, including medals, photographs, paintings, posters, news clippings and other artifacts connected to the Code Talker story. Like a museum curator, Sam, with great pride and meticulous care, explains about each piece. His treasured pieces are the jar, which contains white sand, seashells, and the tear-stained handkerchief from Guam and the Silver Medal.

Lessons Learned

Sam shared how he has tried to live a life to honor the Lord Jesus Christ, his family and family heritage, his friends, and his people and nation - in that order. He has found peace, joy and contentment in life. He seeks to stay true to the basic philosophies of helping those in need and of refraining from having bad thoughts about others or from cursing or judging others. He is redeemed and confident in the grace of Jesus Christ. After out-living his great-grandfather, he will see his rewards in heaven. In the meantime as long as God, the Creator of the Heavens and Earth, continues to give him the strength, he will carry out his mission to share the story of the Code Talker, the Navajo Nation and Jesus Christ. He reminds those he visits how very blessed he is to have such a loving wife in Malula and a family and community who love him. Though he wishes he would have understood the importance of faith and family at an earlier age, he has concluded that life's trials and struggles may be the very thing one needs to endure inorder to awaken the soul to what should be the focus and passions in life.

Reflections

On our trip to Buffalo Mountain and eventually Window Rock, I recall how Sam told the story of Shiprock, the Navajo creation story that tells how his people were created. He spoke of the significance of the four Navajo colors and winds, the dependence on natural resources supplied by the land, and the provisions God has provided such as corn and livestock. It is a story of good and evil connected with Shiprock and the reasons why the magnificent rock formation is sacred to the Navajo people. He told about the "monster" that was eating the Navajo people and how the twin warriors bravely slayed the monster, therefore preventing the slaughter of the Navajo people. Though the creation story of the monster is an ancient one, there are still monsters that threaten to destroy the soul of Samuel's people and he continues to fight against these monsters with warrior-like passion. Sam can easily spend an hour explaining the Navajo creation story and still not cover all of the significance of this ancient, yet relevant story. Whenever he has opportunity, he tells this story along with several other traditional stories. He especially enjoys speaking to younger generations of Navajos. He feels compelled to do his part to make sure the youth are taught about their cultural heritage. Audiences are fascinated with the heroic and compelling tales of the Code Talkers, and this has become his platform for sharing the heart and soul of the Navajo people. The Navajo Code Talker story is only a small chapter in the rich Navajo Nation narrative, a narrative that includes a strong foundation, the endurance of hardships and the constant battle to maintain their rich heritage, and the continued quest for generational relevance. While Sam is proud and honored to talk about the Code Talkers, his passion is to make sure that Navajo ways and traditions are not lost in the next generation.

After many conversations with Sam, I was moved by his devotion to God, family and community. His faith is grounded in Jesus Christ. Though some would see a conflict between the Christian faith and the Navajo tradition, Sam's view is different. He has heard the criticism that the Christian faith is a white man's religion. He understands why some would have those opinions, given some of the questionable and inhuman treatments that were administered by those who introduced Christianity to the tribe. His reminder would be to refrain from judging anyone who is ignorant of and/or are not living the truth of the Word of God and Christ's example. Some people will choose to misrepresent or distort their culture, traditions and beliefs. This choice does not nullify the truth.

There is one practice in the Navajo Christian Church that concerns Sam greatly. This is the church's support of the use of peyote, a native plant. When dyed and smoked, peyote causes the user to hallucinate. While he understands some of the medicinal and traditional reasons for the use of peyote in the Navajo culture, he sees no positive use of it in his walk with God. He does not need any substance for God to reveal Himself. He believes God freely gives insight, wisdom and knowledge through the Holy Spirit without the need for any psychoactive substances.

Samuel has experienced the workings of Christ in and through the Navajo ways. To this day, he cannot explain how God worked a miracle using the traditional ways to heal him when he could not walk. He admits there are some areas of tension with some of the medicines and traditional ways that do not align perfectly with the traditional Christian understanding, but he sees nothing that prohibits him from having a personal relationship with his Lord and Savior. He has put aside denominational/religious arguments and has chosen to put his faith in the person of Christ and the Word of God. He believes that if a person looks at how God chose to reveal Himself to the world, he will see that He chose people like himself - hardworking people making a living and loving and serving their family and community. God revealed Himself on the night Jesus was born, through Christ, a non-Caucasian man, to a non-Caucasian people who were sheep herdsmen with little earthly wealth, not to wealthy dignitaries asleep in warm palace beds. He intentionally chose twelve men, and later many others, who were fisherman, tentmakers, homemakers and other common, everyday hard-working people. He handpicked and called others from diverse nationalities, genders and racial backgrounds to establish His kingdom. He mercifully and graciously chose people like Samuel, "herdsman, in the desert and under the stars, tending their sheep by night."

Words of Wisdom

Sam continues his quest to do his part to make a positive difference within his family, community and the Navajo Nation because he believes in the power of language. The proper care and loving use of language can still defeat enemies today. In the Pacific during WWII, it was not the Navajo language that was such an effective weapon for success on the battlefield; it was the way the Navajo language was used. The code for life is not the Navajo code, nor that of any other language. The code is in the proper use of the language through encouragement, admiration, acknowledgment and love. This is the key to defeating the monsters between people. The secret of the code was not lost at the end of WWII, it was the correct use of the code with each other, which we have lost. Samuel has wisely taught me and, no doubt, many others that "language" can defeat the enemies (monsters) of our soul through the Word of God and prayer.

Finally:

"Our story is the greatest legacy that we'll leave to our godchild, Kenneth Don Lee. It's the longest-lasting legacy we'll leave for the next generation on a level we could only imagine. Kenneth Don Lee was born on May 22, 2000, at Shiprock Northern Navajo Medical Center to Kenneth Lee (father) and Martha Lee (mother). Grandfather Samuel F. Sandoval was the first to hold the baby boy in his arms when he came into this world. Kenneth Don has always been Grandpa's tail ... he knows the ins and out of our marriage and our personal, daily life as husband and wife."

"My voice was heard on sea, on land and heaven above."
             (Sam ends his talks with theses words.)

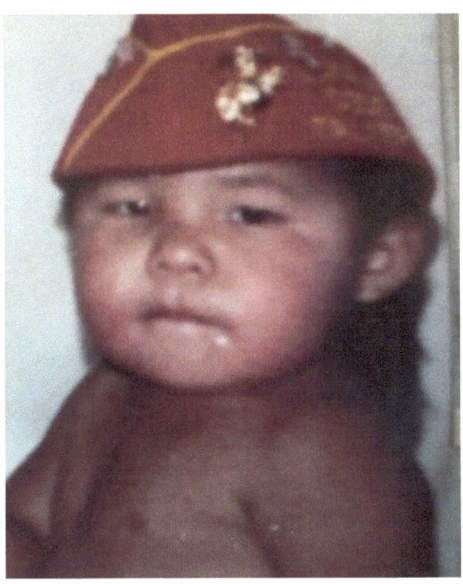

Kenneth Don Lee (Family photo)

The front of the Sandoval home in Shiprock. (JCCC photo)

A portion of Sam's Code Talker collection. (JCCC photo)

Sam explaining the Navajo Code. (JCCC photo)

Sam at the Navajo Code Talker Memorial, Window Rock, AZ. (JCCC photo)

Sam's brick just below the Code Talker statue at the Navajo Code Talker Memorial. (JCCC photo)

Film crew on location during the shooting of *The Heart of a Warrior*. (JCCC photo)

Shiprock. (JCCC photo)

Samuel F. Sandoval dressed in the official Navajo Code Talker uniform. (JCCC photo)

www.ingramcontent.com/pod-product-compliance
Lightning Source LLC
Chambersburg PA
CBHW041627220426
43663CB00004B/92